To the Reader:

Scientology® applied religious philosophy contains pastoral counseling procedures intended to assist an individual to gain greater knowledge of self. The mission of the Church of Scientology is a simple one: to help the individual achieve greater self-confidence and personal integrity, thereby enabling him to really trust and respect himself and his fellow man. The attainment of the benefits and goals of Scientology philosophy requires each individual's dedicated participation, as only through his own efforts can he achieve these.

This book is based on the religious literature and works of the Scientology Founder, L. Ron Hubbard. It is presented to the reader as a part of the record of his personal research into life, and the application of same by others, and should be construed only as a written report of such research and not as a statement of claims made by the Church or the Founder.

Scientology philosophy and its forerunner, Dianetics® spiritual healing technology, as practiced by the Church, address only the "thetan" (spirit). Although the Church, as are all churches, is free to engage in spiritual healing, it does not, as its primary goal is increased spiritual awareness *for all. For this reason, the Church does not wish to accept individuals who desire treatment of physical or mental illness but prefers to refer these to qualified specialists of other organizations who deal in these matters.*

The Hubbard® Electrometer is a religious artifact used in the Church confessional. It in itself does nothing, and is used by ministers only, to assist parishioners in locating areas of spiritual distress or travail.

We hope the reading of this book is only the first stage of a personal voyage of discovery into this new and vital world religion.

Church of Scientology International

This Book Belongs to:

_____

_____

(Date)

child dianetics

child dianetics

L. Ron Hubbard

Bridge
PUBLICATIONS, INC.

Published in the U.S.A. by
Bridge Publications, Inc.
4751 Fountain Avenue
Los Angeles, California 90029

ISBN 0-88404-421-1

Published in other countries by
New Era Publications International, ApS
Store Kongensgade 55
1264 Copenhagen K, Denmark

ISBN 87-7336-608-0

*D*ianetics spiritual healing technology is man's most advanced school of the mind. *Dianetics* means "through the soul" (from Greek *dia*, through, and *noos*, soul). *Dianetics* is further defined as "what the soul is doing to the body." It is a way of handling the energy of which life is made in such a way as to bring about a greater efficiency in the organism and in the spiritual life of the individual.

Important Note

In reading this book, be very certain you never go past a word you do not fully understand.

The only reason a person gives up a study or becomes confused or unable to learn is because he or she has gone past a word that was not understood.

The confusion or inability to grasp or learn comes AFTER a word that the person did not have defined and understood.

Have you ever had the experience of coming to the end of a page and realizing you didn't know what you had read? Well, somewhere earlier on that page you went past a word that you had no definition for or an incorrect definition for.

Here's an example. "It was found that when the crepuscule arrived the children were quieter and when it was not present, they were much livelier." You see what happens. You think you don't understand the whole idea, but the inability to understand came entirely from the one word you could not define, *crepuscule*, which means twilight or darkness.

It may not only be the new and unusual words that you will have to look up. Some commonly used words can often be misdefined and so cause confusion.

This datum about not going past an undefined word is the most important fact in the whole subject of study. Every subject you have taken up and abandoned had its words which you failed to get defined.

Therefore, in studying this book be very, very certain you never go past a word you do not fully understand. If the material becomes confusing or you can't seem to grasp it, there will be a word just earlier that you have not understood. Don't go any further, but go back to BEFORE you got into trouble, find the misunderstood word and get it defined.

Definitions

As an aid to the reader, words most likely to be misunderstood have been defined in footnotes the first time they occur in the text. Words sometimes have several meanings. The footnote definitions in this book only give the meaning that the word has as it is used in the text. Other definitions for the word can be found in a dictionary.

A glossary including all the footnote definitions is at the back of this book. This glossary is not meant as a substitute for a dictionary.

The *Dianetics and Scientology Technical Dictionary* and *Modern Management Technology Defined* are both invaluable tools for the student. They are available from your nearest Scientology church or mission, or directly from the publisher.

Contents

Introduction

C*hild Dianetics* is being published to fill a need.

It is staff collected and staff written except for this introduction and that, necessarily, takes quite a while. Dianetics meanwhile has advanced considerably. The "theta–MEST" theory,[1] Validation Processing,[2] MEST Processing[3] and other developments can spot considerable additional light on Child Dianetics. This book is published because of demand, not because it is up to date.

---

1. **theta–MEST theory:** the theory which states that theta, or life, is impinged upon the physical universe and that these two things together, theta and MEST interacting, give us life forms.

2. **Validation Processing:** processing in which the auditor, at least for one session, concentrates exclusively on the theta side of lock chains, not allowing the preclear to run any but analytical moments on any given subject. When the preclear encounters too much entheta on a given chain, the auditor takes him to analytical moments on another subject (which moments constitute, of course, a parallel chain to the locks on that subject) obtained from the file clerk. During this type of processing somatics will turn on and off, sometimes severely, but the auditor ignores them, and keeps bringing the preclear back to analytical (not necessarily pleasure) moments.

3. **MEST Processing:** processing which deals with the root of aberration and physical condition by calling for physical manifestation rather than words. MEST Processing reaches into that strata underlying language and processes the individual in the physical universe. It processes his communication lines directed toward matter, energy, space and time.

The main problem with children is not so much how to process them into sanity as it is to live with them. The adult is the problem in child raising, not the child. For the adult we have *Science of Survival* and *Self Analysis*. An adult has certain rights around children which the children and modern adults rather tend to ignore. A good, stable adult with love and tolerance in his heart is about the best therapy a child can have.

The main consideration in raising children is the problem of training them without breaking them. The Jesuits[4] had a system which is reported to have been workable but the system perished with the Jesuits. In contradistinction, the American Medical Association—an organization devoted to efforts to control the practices of doctors—lately came out with a pamphlet, a masterpiece of nonsense, which was called "How to Control Your Child." That's just what you don't want to do. You want to raise your child in such a way that you don't have to control him, so that he will be in full possession of himself at all times. Upon that depends his good behavior, his health, his sanity.

The good ex-barbers[5] to the contrary, children are not dogs. They can't be trained like dogs are trained. They are not controllable items. They are, and let's not overlook the point, men and women. A *child* is not a special species of animal distinct from man. A child is a man or a woman who has not attained full growth.

---

4. **Jesuits:** members of a Roman Catholic religious order (Society of Jesus) founded by Ignatius of Loyola in 1534. Mainly a missionary order, the Jesuits used education as its primary means of propagating their beliefs.

5. **ex-barbers:** those who were once barbers. This is a satirical reference to the fact that modern physicians, and therefore the American Medical Association, are descended from barbers. The barber was the original surgeon, performing mainly the pulling of teeth and bloodletting (in addition to the usual cutting of beards and hair). The surgeon separated out as a profession directly from the barber's craft, and then the surgeon became a physician.

Any law which applies to the behavior of men and women applies to children.

How would you like to be pulled and hauled and ordered about and restrained from doing whatever you wanted to do? You'd resent it. The only reason a child "doesn't" resent it is because he's small. You'd half murder somebody who treated you, an adult, with the orders, contradiction and disrespect given to the average child. The child doesn't strike back because he isn't big enough. He gets your floor muddy, interrupts your nap, destroys the peace of the home instead. If he had equality with you in the matter of rights, he'd not ask for this "revenge." This "revenge" is standard child behavior.

A child has a right to his self-determinism.[6] You say that if he is not restrained from pulling things down on himself, running into the road, etc., etc., he'll be hurt. What are you as an adult doing to make that child live in rooms or an environment where he *can* be hurt? The fault is yours, not his, if he breaks things.

The sweetness and love of a child is preserved only so long as he can exert his own self-determinism. You interrupt that and to a degree you interrupt his life.

There are only two reasons why a child's right to decide for himself has to be interrupted—the fragility and danger of his environment and *you*. For you work out on him the things that were done to you, regardless of what you think.

There are two courses you can take. Give the child leeway in

---

6. **self-determinism:** that state of being wherein the individual can or cannot be controlled by his environment according to his own choice. He is confident about any and all abilities or talents he may possess. He is confident in his interpersonal relationships. He reasons but does not need to react.

an environment he can't hurt, which can't badly hurt him and which doesn't greatly restrict his space and time. And you can clean up your own aberrations[7] to a point where your tolerance equals or surpasses his lack of education in how to please you.

When you give a child something, it's *his*. It's not still yours. Clothes, toys, quarters, what he has been given, *must remain under his exclusive control*. So he tears up his shirt, wrecks his bed, breaks his fire engine. It's *none of your business*. How would you like to have somebody give you a Christmas present and then tell you, day after day thereafter, what you are to do with it and even punish you if you failed to care for it the way the donor thinks? You'd wreck that donor and ruin that present. You know you would. The child wrecks your nerves when you do it to him. That's revenge. He cries. He pesters you. He breaks your things. He "accidentally" spills his milk. And he wrecks the possession *on purpose* about which he is so often cautioned. Why? Because he is fighting for his own self-determinism, his own right to own and make his weight felt on his environment. This "possession" is another channel by which he can be controlled. So he has to fight the possession and the controller.

Doubtless, the worthy ex-barbers were so poorly raised they think *control* is the ne plus ultra[8] of child raising. If you want to control your child, simply break him into complete apathy and he'll be as obedient as any hypnotized half-wit. If you want to know how to control him, get a book on dog training, name the child Rex and teach him first to "fetch" and then to "sit up" and then to bark for his food. You can train a child that way. Sure you can. But it's your hard luck if he turns out to be a blood-letter.

---

7. **aberrations:** departures from rational thought or behavior. From the Latin, *aberrare,* to wander from; Latin, *ab,* away, *errare,* to wander. It means basically to err, to make mistakes, or more specifically to have fixed ideas which are not true. Aberration is opposed to sanity, which would be its opposite.

8. *ne plus ultra: (Latin)* the utmost limit, or the highest point of perfection.

Only don't be half-hearted about it. Simply *train* him. "Speak, Roger!" "Lie down!" "Roll over!"

Of course, you'll have a hard time of it. This—a slight medical oversight—is a *human being*. You better charge right in and do what you can to break him into apathy quickly. A club is best. Tying him in a closet without food for a few days is fairly successful. The best recommended tactic, however, is simply to use a straitjacket and muffs on him until he is so docile and imbecilic that he couldn't be trained in anything but psychology* for a profession. I'm warning you that it's going to be tough; it will be tough because man became king of the beasts only because he couldn't as a species be licked. He doesn't easily go into an obedient apathy like dogs do. *Men* own *dogs* because men are self-determined and dogs aren't.

The reason people started to confuse children with dogs and to start training children with force lies in the field of psychology. The psychologist worked on "principles" as follows:

"Man is evil."

"Man must be trained into being a social animal."

"Man must adapt to his environment."

As these postulates[9] aren't true, psychology doesn't work. And if you ever saw a wreck, it's the child of a professional psychologist. Attention to the world around us instead of to texts somebody thought up after reading somebody's texts, shows us the fallacy of these postulates.

* *A cult which rose and expired in the first half of the twentieth century.* —LRH

---

9. **postulates:** things put there as a reality.

The reason Dianetics does what it does is because Dianetics is based on some workable postulates. Psychology didn't even know you had to have postulates and axioms to have a science — didn't even realize that the above constituted their basic creed. The above is formulated from an inspection of their vast tomes.[10]

The actuality is quite opposite the previous beliefs.

The truth lies in this direction:

Man is basically good.

Only by severe aberration can man be made evil. Severe training drives him into nonsociability.

Man must retain his personal ability to adapt his environment to him to remain sane.

A man is as sane and safe as he is self-determined.

In raising your child, you must avoid "training" him into a social animal. Your child begins by being more sociable, more dignified than you are. In a relatively short time the treatment he gets so checks[11] him that he revolts. This revolt can be intensified until he is a terror to have around. He will be noisy, thoughtless, careless of possessions, unclean — anything, in short, which will annoy you. Train him, control him and you'll lose his love. You've lost the child forever that you seek to control and own.

---

10. **tomes:** books, especially very heavy, large or learned books.

11. **checks:** restrains; holds in restraint or control.

Permit a child to sit on your lap. He'll sit there, contented. Now put your arms around him and constrain him to sit there. Do this even though he wasn't even trying to leave. Instantly, he'll squirm. He'll fight to get away from you. He'll get angry. He'll cry. Recall now, he was happy before you started to hold him. (You should actually make this experiment.)

Your efforts to mold, train, control this child in general react on him exactly like trying to hold him on your lap.

Of course you will have difficulty if this child of yours has already been trained, controlled, ordered about, denied his own possessions. In mid-flight, you change your tactics. You try to give him his freedom. He's so suspicious of you, he will have a terrible time trying to adjust. The transition period will be terrible. But at the end of it you'll have a well-ordered, well-trained, social child, thoughtful of you and, very important to you, a child who loves you.

The child who is under constraint, shepherded, handled, controlled, has a very bad anxiety postulated. His parents are survival entities. They mean food, clothing, shelter, affection. This means he wants to be near them. He wants to love them naturally, being their child.

But on the other hand his parents are nonsurvival entities. *His whole being and life depend upon his rights to use his own decision about his movements and his possessions and his body.* Parents seek to interrupt this out of the mistaken idea that a child is an idiot who won't learn unless "controlled." So he has to fight shy, to fight against, to annoy and harass an enemy.

Here is anxiety. "I love them dearly. I also need them. But

they mean an interruption of my ability, my mind, my potential life. What am I going to do about my parents? I can't live with them. I can't live without them. Oh, dear, oh, dear!" There he sits in his rompers[12] running this problem through his head. That problem, that anxiety, will be with him for eighteen years, more or less. And it will half wreck his life.

Freedom for the child means freedom for you. Abandoning the possessions of the child to their fate means eventual safety for the child's possessions.

What terrible willpower is demanded of a parent not to give constant streams of directions to a child! What agony to watch his possessions going to ruin! What upset to refuse to order his time and space!

But it has to be done if you want a well, a happy, a careful, a beautiful, an intelligent child!

Another thing is the matter of contribution. You have no right to deny your child the right to contribute.

A human being feels able and competent only so long as he is permitted to contribute as much or more than he has contributed to him.

A man can over-contribute and feel secure in an environment. He feels insecure the moment he under-contributes, which is to say, gives less than he receives. If you don't believe this, recall a time when everyone else brought something to the party but you didn't. How did you feel?

---

12. **rompers:** a loose, one-piece garment combining a shirt or blouse and short, bloomerlike pants, worn by young children.

A human being will revolt against and distrust any source which contributes to him more than he contributes to it.

Parents, naturally, contribute more to a child than the child contributes back. As soon as the child sees this he becomes unhappy. He seeks to raise his contribution level; failing, he gets angry at the contributing source. He begins to detest his parents. They try to override this revolt by contributing more. The child revolts more. It is a bad dwindling spiral[13] because the end of it is that the child will go into apathy.

You *must* let the child contribute to you. You can't order him to contribute. You can't command him to mow the grass and then think that that's contribution. He has to figure out what his contribution is and then give it. If he hasn't selected it, it isn't his, but only more control.

A baby contributes by trying to make you smile. The baby will show off. A little older he will dance for you, bring you sticks, try to repeat your work motions to help you. If you don't accept those smiles, those dances, those sticks, those work motions in the spirit they are given, you have begun to interrupt the child's contribution. Now he will start to get anxious. He will do unthinking and strange things to your possessions in an effort to make them "better" for you. You scold him. That finishes him.

Something else enters in here. And that is *data*. How can a child possibly know what to contribute to you or his family or

---

13. **dwindling spiral:** a phenomenon of the ARC triangle whereby when one breaks some affinity, a little bit of the reality goes down, and then communication goes down, which makes it impossible to get affinity as high as before; so a little bit more gets knocked off affinity, and then reality goes down, and then communication. This is the dwindling spiral in progress, until it hits the bottom—death—which is no affinity, no communication and no reality.

home *if* he hasn't any idea of the working principles on which it runs?

A family is a group with the common goal of group survival and advancement. The child not allowed to contribute or failing to understand the goals and working principles of family life is cast adrift from the family. He is shown he is not part of the family because he can't contribute. So he becomes antifamily— the first step on the road to being antisocial. He spills milk, annoys your guests and yells outside your window in "play." He'll even get sick just to make you work. He is shown to be nothing by being shown that he isn't powerful enough to contribute.

You can do nothing more than accept the smiles, the dances, the sticks of the very young. But as soon as a child can understand, he should be given the whole story of the family operation.

What is the source of his allowance? How come there is food? Clothes? A clean house? A car?

Daddy works. He expends hours and brains and brawn and for this he gets money. The money, handed over at a store, buys food. A car is cared for because of money scarcity. A calm house and care of Daddy means Daddy works better and that means food and clothes and cars.

Education is necessary because one earns better after he has learned.

Play is necessary in order to give a reason for hard work.

Give him the whole picture. If he's been revolting, he may keep right on revolting. But he'll eventually come around. If he can't get the point in a calm talk about it, you'll simply have to get an auditor[14] to process him a little bit because you went a long ways too far if he can't get the point in a calm talk about it.

First of all a child needs *security*. Part of that security is understanding. Part of it is a code of conduct which is invariable. What is against the law today can't be ignored tomorrow.

You can actually punish a child physically to defend your rights, so long as he owns what he owns and can contribute to you and work for you.

Adults have rights. He ought to know this. A child has as his goal, growing up. If an adult doesn't have more rights, why grow up? Who the devil would be an adult in this year of our Lord anyway?

The child has a duty toward you. He has to be able to take care of you; not an illusion that he is, but actually. And you have to have patience to allow yourself to be cared for sloppily until by sheer experience itself—not by your directions—he learns how to do it well. Care for the child?—nonsense! He's probably got a better grasp of immediate situations than you have, you beaten-up adult. Only when he's almost psychotic[15]

---

14. **auditor:** a person trained and qualified in applying Dianetics processes and procedures to individuals for their betterment; called an auditor because *auditor* means *one who listens.*

15. **psychotic:** an individual who is out of contact to a thorough extent with his present-time environment and who does not compute into the future. He may be an acute psychotic wherein he becomes psychotic for only a few minutes at a time and only occasionally in certain environments (as in rages or apathies) or he may be a chronic psychotic, or in a continual disconnection with the future and present. Psychotics who are dramatically harmful to others are considered dangerous enough to be put away. Psychotics who are harmful on a less dramatic basis are no less harmful to their environment and are no less psychotic.

---

with aberration will a child be an accident prone.

You're well and enjoy life because you aren't *owned*. Your American forefathers fought slavery twice—1776 and 1861. You *couldn't* enjoy life if you were shepherded and owned. You'd revolt. And if your revolt was quenched, you'd turn into a subversive. That's what you make out of your child when you own, manage and control him.

Potentially, parent, he's saner than you are and the world is a lot brighter. His sense of values and reality are sharper. Don't dull them. And your child will be a fine, tall, successful human being. Own, control, manage and reject and you'll get the treatment you deserve—subversive revolt.

That's all I can tell you right now. *Self Analysis* is your best pattern of processing to use on a child. Only you ask *him* the questions.

Now, are we going to have a happy house around here or aren't we?

L. Ron Hubbard
Wichita, 1951.

1

Basic Dianetics Principles

1

Basic Dianetics Principles

For centuries many scientists and philosophers have been studying the convolutions of human thinking. The longer the study, the greater their reassurance that we are the possessors of a most complex and challenging instrument called the mind. What they refer to is, since the advent[1] of Dianetics, distinguished as the *analytical mind*.[2]

But describing its behavior did not make the ways of the mind any less baffling. Our knowledge of the actual functioning which takes place when we think continued to be only approximate at best. There were still many unexplained aspects, unknown stimuli[3] and unaccountable factors—until the theory of Dianetics was applied.

The stumbling block, Dianetics proved after twelve years of experimentation, is the fact that we are also the possessors of

1. **advent:** coming or arrival.

2. **analytical mind:** the conscious, aware mind which thinks, observes data, remembers it and resolves problems. It would be essentially the conscious mind as opposed to the unconscious mind. In Dianetics the analytical mind is the one which is alert and aware and the reactive mind simply reacts without analysis.

3. **stimuli:** things that incite to action or exertion or quicken action, feeling, thought, etc.

another mind, the *reactive mind*,[4] which has far greater force and compulsion upon us than the so-called analytical mind. In fact, when brought into play, the reactive mind badgers and bedevils us throughout our entire life span.

Like the analytical mind, the reactive mind is also a mental function. It is a kind of primitive function in that it is a vicious and violent survival mechanism in living organisms.

But the reactive mind does not analyze—it thinks only in terms of identities and similarities, not in both similarities and differences as does the analytical mind. It is strictly a *literal* mind that responds defensively every time something reminds it of a similar painful incident.

The animal mentality, being largely reactive, is a good illustration. Suppose a quietly browsing doe, confident at the moment that no danger lurked nearby, ranged beneath a tree. Suddenly a huge snake dropped down upon her back and terrified her (threatened her survival). The terror would cause her meager analytical faculties to become attenuated[5] or partly unconscious, whereupon her indomitable[6] reactive mind would take over, directing the organism toward survival in a manner deriving from past successful survivals in time of great danger. The impressions received at the time of extreme danger and terror are recorded and filed away for future survival use. Thereafter, that tree and all others resembling it will be associated with the snake threat in the doe's mind. Every time the doe sees such

4. **reactive mind:** that portion of a person's mind which works on a totally stimulus-response basis, which is not under his volitional control and which exerts force and the power of command over his awareness, purposes, thoughts, body and actions. The reactive mind is where engrams are stored. Also called **bank.**

5. **attenuated:** weakened or reduced in force, intensity, effect, quantity or value.

6. **indomitable:** not easily discouraged, defeated or subdued; unyielding; unconquerable.

a tree, the recording of the fearful incident will cause it to shy away on pain of death, for to the reactive mind, pain means death and pleasure means survival.

To civilized human beings, however, the reactive mind has become a leech[7] upon rational behavior. It is the hypothetical cyst[8] which occludes the proper functioning of the analytical mind; it is the root of all our psychosomatic[9] ills, and the barrier which prevents us from attaining the optimum of our thinking abilities and aspirations.

It is remarkable what powerful pressures the reactive mind can exert upon the individual in order to make him obey commands. Even though it is presumably a prosurvival monitor, it cannot analyze and know the *difference* between things.

Thus, if a brindle[10] cow kicked you and inflicted pain while you were making an amateurish attempt to milk her, thenceforward *all* brindle cows would become hateful creatures to you and *all* sunny pastures would restimulate[11] the unconsciousness. You would even reexperience the pain of that kick each time you were restimulated.

Of course, it doesn't make sense, but that's the way the reactive mind works; it can't think things out. And yet, by

---

7. **leech:** one who clings to another for personal gain, especially without giving anything in return, and usually with the implication or effect of exhausting the other's resources; parasite.

8. **cyst:** a small sac in animals or plants, usually containing liquid and diseased matter produced by inflammation. Cysts are often caused by the blocking of some passage, for example in a gland.

9. **psychosomatic:** *psycho* refers to mind and *somatic* refers to body; the term psychosomatic means the mind making the body ill or illnesses which have been created physically within the body by derangement of the mind.

10. **brindle:** having a gray or tawny coat streaked or spotted with a darker color.

11. **restimulate:** trigger; stir up.

means of Dianetics, we have discovered that hundreds of other psychosomatic ills are imposed upon the human body in exactly that crazy way.

What does the reactive mind consist of? It is a kind of storage bank of memory, mostly of unpleasant things done to us from the very first moment of life, but only of those events which happened while we were unconscious or in pain. As such it differs from our previous understanding of the meaning and uses of memory.

Here it is necessary to define memory as a process of *recalling,* at will or in response to appropriate stimuli, impressions previously made on the senses and recorded in the mind. The process of recall is essentially one of *perceiving* these impressions and understanding them; it is an *analytical* process.

What was not before understood by the mental sciences, but can now be demonstrated conclusively by Dianetics, is that yet another file of impressions exists. This other file is one in which impressions are recorded, in a manner and under circumstances that do not permit of *voluntary* recall. These are the impressions recorded by the reactive mind and held there until such times as only that function has occasion to call them into play.

In other words, the reactive mind *reacts* to certain stimuli, but in a manner so incapable of rational explanation, so random and erratic, that it frequently does incalculable harm to the human body and many of its functions.

As previously indicated, the reactive mind records all impressions experienced during moments of unconsciousness or of pain sufficient to lower the perceptive abilities of the analytical mind to a point less than full consciousness. Therefore, before any of these data can affect the individual adversely, it is a condition that it must be activated or "keyed in"[12] by an occurrence in the life of the individual similar to the one originally recorded. From then on the occurrence is capable of being reactivated by every such occurrence as a restimulator.

We have said that the reactive mind records with the implication that the data are filed as obtained, without regard for system or original context. Similar results would be obtained were a tape recorder to be placed in operation upon a busy street corner. Auto horns, crashes, whistles and snatches of conversation would all be found on the tape in replay. No selective mechanism could be devised which would do more than play off that which was recorded.

This is the activity of the reactive mind: recording and replay in response to restimulation. Therefore, when any recording in the reactive mind is caused to replay, the individual responds with a literal interpretation of the content of that particular recording, and literal interpretation can be very, very far removed from implied meaning.

It will be appreciated, then, what startling, ludicrous and even disastrous results may be observed when this nonanalytical, strictly literal mind is restimulated. For example, a pregnant woman trips, falls heavily to the floor; her unborn child is momentarily stunned (unconsciousness). In her terror and concern she cries out, "My baby! I have harmed him, given him a terrible setback! He will never be like other children!" Even though the child is born without any mishaps or disfigurements, yet when during its childhood someone remarks in a manner

---

12. **keyed in:** restimulated. The environment around the awake but fatigued or distressed individual is itself similar to the dormant engram. At that moment the engram becomes active.

intended to be *complimentary,* "He is not like other children," the prenatal incident "keys in" and thereafter he unconsciously *seeks* to be different, sulking in corners, refusing to join with other children in their play or various other normal activities.

This does happen, as can be and has been demonstrated!

Now, a true science not only recognizes the problems in its field, but also offers a method for their solution. As a true science, Dianetics has evolved a method for recognizing and solving these human problems. The method is known as Dianetic processing. The solution is the erasure of those recordings which, when restimulated, cause reactive behavior in the human being.

The individual whose reactive mind bank no longer contains any aberrative incidents is known in Dianetic terminology as a "Clear." But a person who is still undergoing Dianetic processing—either for a relief of psychosomatic pain or discomfort or with the goal in mind of becoming Clear—is called a "preclear."

Dianetic processing is an astonishingly simple technique. The preclear is asked to make himself comfortable and close his eyes. He is then asked to return[13] to a past moment of pleasure. The moment of pleasure is recounted, and by adroit questioning his auditor endeavors to elicit all possible details contained in the incident. This has the effect of acquainting the person with the practicability and process of "going back" or "returning." It also

13. **return:** go into a past period. A person can "send" a portion of his mind to a past period on either a mental or combined mental and physical basis and can reexperience incidents which have taken place in his past in the same fashion and with the same sensations as before.

sharpens his powers of recall, and at the same time allays[14] any doubts he may experience.

He is next asked to go back or return to the first moment of pain or unconsciousness available at the time. What he contacts is called an "engram,"[15] which is the scientific name for an impression upon the organism. Again, adroit questioning aids him to recall details. Several recountings of the incident serve to remove what may be called the "charge"[16] on this incident, thus restoring to the analytical mind that vital energy heretofore required to endure or live with the disruptive content of the engram.

From here the preclear is led by the auditor into further, more deeply embedded incidents, the ultimate aim of which is to contact, and erase, the hidden memories of all such aberrative events that may be present in the "bank." These data in the reactive mind are actually contacted with the aid of the auditor, whose assistance is required to direct the preclear into the most likely lines of attack.

It may be surprising, but the data are all recorded there in the reactive mind, waiting to be contacted, erased and placed by

14. **allays:** puts (fear, doubt, suspicion, anger, etc.) to rest; calms; quiets.

15. **engram:** a mental image picture which is a recording of an experience containing pain, unconsciousness and a real or fancied threat to survival. It is a recording in the reactive mind of something which actually happened to an individual in the past and which contained pain and unconsciousness, both of which are recorded in the mental image picture called an engram. It must, by definition, have impact or injury as part of its content. These engrams are a complete recording, down to the last accurate detail, of every perception present in a moment of partial or full unconsciousness.

16. **charge:** harmful energy or force accumulated and stored within the reactive mind, resulting from the conflicts and unpleasant experiences that a person has had. Auditing discharges this charge so that it is no longer there to affect the individual.

the auditing process into standard or nonaberrative memory. The process thus releases vital energy needed for the better functioning of the analytical mind. It is obvious, then, that with every such release the analytical mind recovers more and more of its original, endowed potential for clear and rational thinking.

Children, of course, are to a large degree subject to the vagaries[17] of the reactive mind. Many children are morose and sullen much of the time, reluctant to mingle with the more active children of the neighborhood.

Others are "problem" children who scream, kick, bite and scratch at the slightest provocation. And others find their way into public institutions such as juvenile homes and the dreaded reform schools, all because they are obeying hidden commands contained in the reactive mind bank.

Because of their age and limited maturity, children must be regarded as a special branch of Dianetics. In recognition of the special considerations involved, a research program designed to find the best Dianetic approach to the problems of their processing has been conducted during the year following publication of *Dianetics: The Modern Science of Mental Health.* The resultant discoveries cannot be ignored by parents or persons who share responsibility of rearing children and genuinely have the welfare of their youngsters at heart.

17. **vagaries:** unpredictable or erratic actions, occurrences, courses or instances.

2

Our Greatest
Problem

2

Our Greatest Problem

What do you consider the greatest problem in each individual's life? Think it over for a moment. Is it war, famine, disease? Is it love, hate, money or social position? Or might it be that process which we all go through, the process of finding out what it means to find ourselves? Does the latter seem, if not the *greatest* problem to you, at least one of the greatest problems which every person faces? Dianetics has found it to be the root problem.

The aim of Dianetic processes is the *Clear*. One of the characteristics which is attributed to the Clear is that of self-determinism. But to be self-determined one must have a realization of what one wishes to accomplish and what one can do best. The individual arrives at the answers to these problems partly through experience and partly through what we in Dianetics call B.P. or "basic personality."[1]

In Dianetics, however, we recognize that conditioning which comes from engrams can cause an individual to be forced away

---

1. **basic personality:** the individual himself. The basic individual is not a buried unknown or a different person, but an intensity of all that is best and most able in the person.

from living in accordance with his basic personality. This can result from engram commands to behave in certain ways, from valence[2] shifts, or from ally computations.[3] Therefore, by no means is the basic personality always realized.

But what causes these deviations? How do they come about? Engrams are "laid in" during the prenatal period. It is then that the prenatal engrams are keyed in and begin to exert their negative influence. It is also during this time that sympathy computations[4] are formed and ally computations are ordered into effect. Childhood illnesses and operations occur during this time and are of considerable importance. It is very often found that a somatic shut-off[5] occurs during a tonsillectomy; or at least it is at this time that the initial key-in is made. Grief shut-offs are found in this area also, with Mother saying, "Don't cry, everything will be all right." This phrase is obviously rather vicious if it feeds into the reactive mind, for it says that if one doesn't ever cry, everything will *necessarily* be all right. It is doubtful that an "everything all right" condition ever has been or ever can be any

---

2. **valence:** personality. The term is used to denote the borrowing of the personality of another. A valence is a substitute for self taken on after the fact of lost confidence in self. A preclear "in his father's valence" is acting as though he were his father.

3. **ally computations:** little more than mere idiot calculations that anyone who is a friend can be kept a friend only by approximating the conditions wherein the friendship was realized. They are *computations* on the basis that one can only be safe in the vicinity of certain people and that one can only be in the vicinity of certain people by being sick or crazy or poor and generally disabled.

4. **sympathy computations:** computations which make the patient "want to be sick." Sickness has a high survival value says the reactive mind, so it tailors up a body to be sick. For example, if a patient had a tough engramic background, then broke his leg and got sympathy, he thereafter tends to go around with a simulated broken leg—arthritis, etc., etc.

5. **somatic shut-off:** a condition wherein a somatic may be shut off in an incident or elsewhere, either by earlier command or late by painful emotion. There is a whole species of commands which *shut off* pain and emotion simultaneously: this is because the word *feel* is homonymic. "I can't feel anything" is the standard, but the command varies widely and is worded in a great many ways.

---

person's undeviating experience. But that is what that engram promises and demands, and if it doesn't come to pass, as it frequently can't, heaven help the poor child, mother or anybody else within his environment.

Let us depart from the specific for a moment and generalize. What is it that happens during childhood? It is not enough to accept that it is the period during which the child grows up. In our society it is that most crucial period during which the individual learns what may be termed basic behavior patterns. These are difficult to change in later life and their origins, because of the initial basis on which they are founded, may very well be completely forgotten. We might say that this is the period during which the child learns, from what he is taught and from experimentation, the means with which he is to express himself. The means he is compelled to use may range from the grossly inadequate to those of greatest assistance to him. In short, we might say that childhood is the period during which the basic methods of self-expression are formed.

Next in importance is the period of late childhood, roughly from six to twelve years. In our society this period is given over greatly to the acquisition of information. It is also devoted, from a slightly different viewpoint, to the compelled learning of data. Dianetics is inclined to question the advisability of this latter occupation. It appears that it might be more advantageous, both from the standpoint of mental health and from the standpoint of the correctness of information which the child assimilates, to teach the child *how* to think before teaching him *what* to think. Child instruction today is largely a matter of wrong emphasis. Dianetically, it would seem that the emphasis should be placed on the *how* rather than the *what* of learning and thinking.

Perhaps we should review some of the reasons for the position we take. In the first place, let's examine what we mean by the "reactive" and the "analytical" minds. The reactive mind, as such, does not appear to be a "mind" in the thinking sense of the word. The reactive mind is primarily a stockpile of painful, unconscious experiences. The material of these experiences appears to be impinged upon a low level of analytical ability. From the functional standpoint, what we refer to as the "thinking" of the reactive mind appears to be a low-level computation on the part of an almost completely shut-down analyzer. It would seem that something of the primary man's tendency to think and speak in terms of identities is carried over by recapitulation[6] into the development of the child's inquisitive sense of being and reality. He first tends to think in terms of identities. This seems to be an initial step toward his realization of differences. Things similar are the same, things different are absolutely different. Because of this tendency on the part of the child, it seems to us that the more rapidly we can influence the child into a multi-valued mode of thinking, the more rapidly he will relinquish identity thinking, and the less effect "reactive" thinking will have upon his mental and physiological functioning.

There is another factor which is important in the child's thinking processes. The child appears to be "closer" to his engrams. By "closer" we mean that he has not had the advantages of time and analytical experience necessary to remove himself from the effect of his engrams. As a very general observation on this feature of the child's thinking, it might be said that the child's sense of reality and affinity[7] with reality have not been built upon extensive experience, and it is therefore difficult for

---

6. **recapitulation:** the theory that the stages an organism passes through during its embryonic development repeat the evolutionary stages of structural change in its ancestral lineage.

7. **affinity:** degree of liking or affection or lack of it. Affinity is a tolerance of distance. A great affinity would be a tolerance of or liking of close proximity. A lack of affinity would be an intolerance of or dislike of close proximity. Affinity is one of the components of understanding.

him to separate what is happening to him as a result of his own past experience from what is happening to him as a result of the present situation in which he finds himself.

It would seem that analytical experience acts as a sort of elevator in which the "I" organization rises as the analytical mind collects experience. The "I" organizes this experience in terms of greater and greater complexity as the individual matures, and this complexity acts as a buffer to engram commands. However, there also appears to be a great disadvantage in this. As the analyzer gets more and more complex, there is a corresponding increase in the force of the individual's engrams, which consistently cause a misevaluation of experience. And as the misevaluation of experience becomes more *extensive*, there is a greater breakdown in the areas of reality, communication and affinity.

Perhaps the most striking feature of the child's attempt to realize his own personality is his shifting of valences. Using even a fairly small amount of observation, it seems possible to put forth as a tentative statement that a rapid shift of valences is a natural process in the child. He "tries on" pieces of valences as if they were clothes, retaining pieces here and there, discarding others which do not fit him. He constructs and synthesizes a personality out of these pieces of valences in conjunction with his own basic personality.

It seems necessary to digress for a moment and comment that the use of the word "valence" is extremely general here. We mean by the word not only the information about persons which is in engrams, but also the limited analytical data which the child acquires from cowboy movies, from reading about and seeing policemen, firemen, etc. This does not include the concept of valence shift induced by a command or a reactive computation for making the shift; the child may be forced by his reactive thinking to shift valences. However the type of valence shift, or trying on parts of other personalities, which is discussed above, is spontaneous, not compulsive. He *imitates*, but not deliberately.

For the child, the whole problem of "self" is obscure and difficult, but of tremendous importance. Various writers on psychology are constantly delving into the complexities of the subject because it is so basic to the study of the formative mind.

In the field of fiction, Lewis Carroll, creator of the immortal *Alice in Wonderland*, shows in a humorous way how Alice is confronted with this difficulty. In the beginning of the chapter entitled "Advice from a Caterpillar," there is some discussion between Alice and the Caterpillar about this whole question. While it would seem that they do not find their own discussion particularly illuminating, we, being more prepared, can view it more pertinently so:

> *The Caterpillar and Alice looked at each other for some time in silence. At last the Caterpillar took the hookah[8] out of its mouth, and addressed her in a languid, sleepy voice.*
>
> *"Who are YOU?" said the Caterpillar.*
>
> *This was not an encouraging opening for a conversation. Alice replied, rather shyly, "I—I hardly know, Sir, just at present—at least I know who I was when I got up this morning, but I think I must have been changed several times since then."*
>
> *"What do you mean by that?" said the Caterpillar sternly. "Explain yourself."*

---

8. **hookah:** a tobacco pipe of Near Eastern origin with a long, flexible tube by which the smoke is drawn through a jar of water and thus cooled.

"I can't explain MYSELF, I'm afraid, Sir," said Alice, "because I'm not myself, you see."

"I don't see," said the Caterpillar.

"I'm afraid I can't put it more clearly," Alice replied very politely, "for I can't understand it myself to begin with; and being so many different sizes in a day is very confusing."

"It isn't," said the Caterpillar.

"Well, perhaps you haven't found it so yet," said Alice. "But when you have to turn into a chrysalis—you will some day, you know—and then into a butterfly, I should think you'll feel it a little queer, won't you?"

"Not a bit," said the Caterpillar.

"Well, perhaps your feelings may be different," said Alice; "all I know is, it would feel very queer to ME."

"You!" said the Caterpillar contemptuously. "Who are YOU?"

Which brought them back again to the beginning of the conversation.

If we wanted to see what Alice's engrams were, we might indulge in some Dianetic literary criticism; however, it will probably be much more valuable if we accept Carroll—and Alice—on their own terms. In this we can get an amusing but nevertheless telling portrayal of the child's wonderment (and befuddlement) as to what a "self" is. The fact that children are confused by this problem is not surprising; it has also stumped the great philosophers. They have struck boldly at the idea, attempting to enter into the core of the thought, but apparently have never been completely successful, judging from the lack of general acceptance of any one philosopher's opinions on the subject.

However deeply we care to look at this problem, we still find that a great deal of the child's difficulty is much more immediate. We do not have to be very philosophical with the child. A large part of his difficulties lie in things which can be fairly easily resolved. For example, children are not very good semanticists;[9] they have rather narrow vocabularies and are mistaken about the meaning of many things. Reality is a fairly small thing to them. Children go through stages of divorcing themselves from whatever surrounds them. When a child is first born, he has no concept of the point where he stops and other things begin. He learns this gradually, but finds the next difficulty one of determining where his wishes stop and other forces begin. The child does not have, completely, the proper sense of reality for the kind of Dianetic processing done with adults and adolescents; the experiences in children's standard banks[10] are not quite adequate to the problems at hand. But it is possible to have affinity with children—lots of it—so there is a possibility of one element compensating for a lack in the other two. If the child really feels that you are trying to help him, you can do a great deal with him.

This brings us to the problem of how to deal with children. There is no exact procedure to give you that will apply infallibly

---

9. **semanticists:** persons concerned with the meanings or interpretations of the meanings of words, signs, sentences, etc.

10. **standard banks:** recordings of everything perceived throughout the lifetime up to present time by the individual except physical pain, which is not recorded in the analytical mind but is recorded in the reactive mind.

to every child, but a series of games is under development, for one thing, which will give all children a better orientation in the use of language. For instance: "How many meanings can you find for the word that sounds like 'road'?" Block games, etc., which will have orientation in semantics as their aim, are being developed.

Now let us take up the question of how children "return." Children seem to look on returning to painful incidents merely as more unpleasant experience, and are unable to see far enough in the future to make returning worthwhile. To the very young, the concepts of reduction[11] and restimulation are too advanced; the only exception so far is the case of chronic physically painful restimulation. When the child suffers constantly from stomachaches, dizzy spells or other complaints that annoy him repeatedly, he will be eager to try anything that promises him relief. Even in this case, however, the child must be constantly reminded that he is being helped when he tells the auditor about the first stomachache, the first dizzy spell, and so on. He can and will feel the somatics only if he is not frightened by them.

Here we come to another big obstacle to returning in children, one that can be overcome only by a friendly attitude and reliability on the part of the auditor. That obstacle is fear. Children do not understand time well; to them the past is jumbled up with the present, and is still as real as today. They fear that yesterday with its pain and terror could happen all over again tomorrow; they fear that returning to a time of pain will bring the experience back in reality. These seem to be natural fears, born of the child's lack of analytical experience with the world. The only apparent solution is education of the children in the Dianetic process.

---

11. **reduction:** the act of taking all the charge or pain out of an incident.

Each child should understand as fully as he can where he came from and what it was like before he was born. He should know what to expect from somatics, and what to expect when he runs the somatics over and over. In short, he must have a fairly good concept of what he and his auditor are doing.

The mere concept of Dianetics, however, is not enough. Children appeal strongly to their authorities. They must have adults they can believe in and trust, whose world they can rely on. If the auditor should make a slip, like telling the child that birth won't hurt him much when he returns to it, the child will be expecting perhaps a mild squeeze or nothing at all. Pain to him is not relative to other pain, but to how he perceives it while it is going on. If he is depressed and tired, he will be less liable to "take"[12] somatics, and the auditor should be aware of this. The auditor must give the child some idea of what his forthcoming experience is going to be like, but he must try not to under-estimate this, because of the risk of losing affinity for a time. This prediction is not easy, and affinity is often lost because of mistakes in guessing the child's ability to perceive pain. Loss of affinity must be run immediately as a lock,[13] and processing must be stopped until the affinity has been reestablished. Running a child who has lost his faith in the auditor's omniscience[14] is inviting dub-in.[15] An auditor hasn't known frustration until he

12. **take:** to endure or submit to with equanimity or without an appreciable weakening of one's resistance.

13. **lock:** a mental image picture of a nonpainful but disturbing experience the person has had, which depends for its force on earlier secondaries and engrams which the experience has restimulated (stirred up).

14. **omniscience:** quality or state of having complete or unlimited knowledge, awareness or understanding; perceiving all things.

15. **dub-in:** unknowingly created mental pictures that appear to have been a record of the physical universe but are, in fact, only altered copies of the time track. It is a phrase out of the motion-picture industry of putting a sound track on top of something that isn't there.

has run a child halfway through a painful experience only to find that a happy ending has been tacked on to it.

Children seem to be able to take the valence of people they are with. Auditors can observe children in the auditor's valence even when the child and the auditor are playing together. This effect seems to occur most often in cases containing much terror, but has been observed even in normal children. The less affinity the child has with adults at home, the more easily he can take the valence of one with whom he does have affinity.

Another thing which is important is to track down dramatizations[16] and get them out as much as possible. In connection with this, it is necessary to counsel the parents on how to avoid restimulation of their children.

If a child is multivalent, it is difficult to determine who he is from one minute to the next. Work on such a child is done almost completely through affinity. He has at least four different valences which he goes into, one after another. He has little reality sense and a circuit which says that only *he* is the one talking. Greater progress is made with this child as affinity between him and his auditor increases.

It is quite possible that use can be made of the natural tendency of the child (if it is that) to *play* in other valences, by giving him valences which are more to his benefit, and certainly more to the benefit of society, than gangsters, tough cops, two-valued cowboys, etc. There have been continuous arguments about the effects of movies on children, the viciousness of some

---

16. **dramatizations:** duplications of engramic content, entire or in part, by an aberree (aberrated person) in his present-time environment. Aberrated conduct is entirely dramatization. When dramatizing, the individual is like an actor playing his dictated part and going through a whole series of irrational actions.

of the comic books, and now the concern revolves around television. With Dianetics we begin to get some insight into why we have felt that there were certain bad effects from these forms of amusement. The valences they get into is a matter of grave concern. It is not a problem for children alone; there are some mighty young adolescents who wear whiskers.

It is hoped that Dianetically sound programs may be instituted to supply useful, educational valences from which children can pick, a concern based on some of the aberration already found in children, most illustrative of which are the "Junior cases."[17] They are still Junior cases when they are fifty, but to be so they must have been Junior cases earlier. The progress of such cases depends somewhat upon the rate at which the engrams were keyed in. A good example of how a Junior case is created is the following: after her divorce, the mother says to her child, a Junior, "Now you are the little man of the house."

It is not surprising that children seem to be similar to psychotics and schizophrenics.[18] The child may play that he is a butterfly, a horse, a box—almost anything. His imagination runs rampant[19] and as a result he looks, in the creation of some of his fantasies, much like a psychotic. The difference is that the child may be doing this as an exercise, whereas the psychotic does it because he must. However, if the child can't stop being a butterfly, then we have a child with aberration. He is stuck in the butterfly's valence.

---

17. **Junior cases:** cases which have the characteristic of sharing the same name as a parent. Let's say the father's name was George and the patient's name was George, the engram bank takes George to mean George and that is identity thought deluxe. Mother says, "I hate George!" "That means Junior," says the engram, though Mother meant Father.

18. **schizophrenics:** *(psychiatry)* originally meaning *split mind,* it has come to denote a psychiatric classification of people whose thoughts and emotions are disassociated from each other.

19. **rampant:** in full sway; prevailing or unchecked.

When the child is swapping valences and wants to be a butterfly, a flower or a cowboy, there is probably nothing wrong. When he gets hung up in one of these valences, we have a problem on our hands. It is the same thing when he gets stuck in one of the family valences or when he has the command, "You're just like all the rest of the family," or "You're just like your father."

A child stuck in a valence very early in his life does not have such a difficult problem, although he may have the psychosomatic illnesses of the person he is being. Probably he would only dramatize a great deal and would have his analyzer turned off most of the time. But the person who is stuck in one valence and suddenly becomes stuck in another at the same time has a greater problem. If he is able to make a synthesis of these valences, perhaps he can make an adjustment; but when this happens to an older person it presents a great deal of conflict. The following is a partly hypothetical example:

> A Junior case detested his father and so went into his mother's valence. He had commands, however, to be like his father. He found it very difficult to deal with reality, and was diagnosed by a psychologist as a split personality. He was also diagnosed as a manic-depressive,[20] but there is little credence[21] to this diagnosis. He was depressed because he couldn't make up his mind.

Children, too, have these problems, particularly in a violently emotional family where it is necessary to their security to have a strong ally. The way to have a strong ally is to get into the

---

20. **manic-depressive:** is an individual who, because of a phrase or an effort or a restimulation—no more and no less—climbs way up the Tone Scale; and he hits a small peak and then dives off it again and goes on with the engram.

21. **credence:** belief as to the truth of something.

---

loser's valence (feel how he feels) and for protection seek to gain the winner of the argument as an ally. You play the necessary part or you build valences with those things which the ally likes best, and then you become them so you have the ally. Example:

Cousin Mary comes to visit the child, Betty, and her family. Mary is a little older and is always very helpful to Betty's mother. Betty is not quite ready to take up such things, but as soon as Mary goes away Mother starts talking about how wonderful it was to have Cousin Mary around because she always helped with the work. The child, if the family situation is an insecure one, is apt to feel that she must go into Cousin Mary's valence in order to retain Mother as an ally.

It must not be forgotten that an ally and a friend may very easily be confused in a child's mind. A child has to have the help of others in order to survive. The loss of an ally is a major catastrophe for the child. The slightest emotional rejection of a child by an ally is an acute threat to the child's survival, particularly if the child is already insecure.

Another thing which is encountered in working with children is the fact that the child *must* obey his parents. When an auditor first fired: "Do you have to do what your mother told you *now?*" at a child, in an attempt to break an aberrative command on a flash-answer[22] basis, he was dumbfounded as to what to do with the immediate yes! answer. In short, the problem can be formulated in this way: for the child to disobey his parents is an actual survival risk of no small proportion.

The only way to get around that is to have secure children

---

22. **flash-answer:** of or characteristic of a first flash response. The *flash answer* is an instantaneous reply, the first thing that flashes into the preclear's mind at the snap of the auditor's fingers.

---

who understand that they are valued for being themselves. Dianetics does not propound this with the idea that children must be allowed to run rampant; they must receive some training. But parents should remember that much of the child's misbehavior is simply a matter of his engrams (which his parents gave him to a large extent) talking back. Pain—intense pain to the child—is driving much of this misbehavior.

A letter was received recently by the Foundation:[23] "We have a little girl who has an older brother, and we know that the little girl has an engram in which her mother says, 'I hope it's a boy; I like boys much better than I like girls.' The girl shows marked tomboy tendencies and tries in every way possible to be like her brother."

The parents wanted to know what they could do. The child is not old enough to run this as an engram. The only possible reply was, "Make it as valuable as possible for the child to be a girl, and be careful not to restimulate her by showing any preference for boys."

Another thing that can be done is to try to blow locks in children. It is very simple, and the child need have no idea what you are doing. The procedure might go: "What were you doing when you bumped your head?" Answer: "I was riding my tricycle." Ask more questions about it, play the incident out, and then go back and play it out again. It is quite effective. Try as consistently as possible to run out locks. If the engrams are not allowed to remain keyed-in, they are ineffective.

There is one other thing to say about valences. If the child happens to be in someone else's valence he has small chance of

23. **Foundation:** the Hubbard Dianetic Research Foundation, the first organization of Dianetics. It was first located in Elizabeth, New Jersey and later in Wichita, Kansas.

ever realizing his own personality, because implicit[24] in the valence is an approach to life, a consistent behavior pattern, etc. The human being is of a tough character and occasionally does manage to break through with some of its own characteristics. But engrams and valences are more often tougher. The point is that being in someone else's valence is obviously not a good thing. The way to help a child is to help him be himself!

24. **implicit:** potential contained (in).

3

Toward a Saner World

3

Toward a Saner World

Contagion of aberration has progressed along the second dynamic[1] to a remarkable degree in our present society. Our first settlers brought the seed of future aberration. As there were certain diseases for which there was no cure, a moral restraint was substituted for this lack.

Such taboos are based upon the premise that something society has done in the past was more painful than beneficial. Prejudice then carries the taboos forward long beyond their time.

Once created, taboos must be enforced. Force is applied against reason. What is aberration but force being applied against reason?

Aberration seems to multiply by geometric progression.[2] It is a spreading, broadening thing rather than a narrow line. Mother's aberrations appear in two of her children and four of

---

1. **second dynamic:** the urge toward survival through sex or children. This dynamic actually has two divisions. Second dynamic (a) is the sexual act itself, and second dynamic (b) is the family unit, including the rearing of children.

2. **geometric progression:** a sequence of terms in which the ratio between any two successive terms is the same, as the progression 1, 3, 9, 27, 81 or 144, 12, 1, $\frac{1}{12}$, $\frac{1}{144}$.

her grandchildren. Father's "idiosyncrasies" follow the same pattern. Within a few generations an entire society is affected.

Only the colonizing of new lands has interrupted this contagion. When a race is facing a new continent and conquering the old inhabitants, it has to raise its necessity level[3] to a very high plateau. It is a tremendous goal to wrest the land from those who already own it, and so long as the impetus carries forth the race is successful, and the contagion within it is cut down considerably.

After a while the goal is accomplished and nearly everything is nicely smoothed out for those who follow. The means of transport and food are available with minimum effort. The government is settled into a rut and suddenly there is a "civilized" nation with no higher goal. At this moment begins the dwindling spiral. Even though the golden age may come for the race at that period, the dwindling spiral of aberration, already begun, goes down and down. The individual's necessity level becomes low and aberrations begin to manifest themselves. The process of contagion sets in.

The customs of society today make it quite fashionable for individuals to have a blocked second dynamic. When an investigator of the stature of Freud[4] studies a social order and decides that just one thing is wrong, it is at least indicative that there is a lot wrong with just that one thing. He was forced to the conclusion that sex is primarily responsible for aberration, and upon examination it is evident that for the past two centuries sex to a greater and greater extent has become taboo.

---

3. **necessity level:** a person's ability to rise above his aberrations when his action is required to handle an immediate and serious threat to his survival.

4. **Freud:** Sigmund Freud (1856–1939), Austrian neurologist, founder of psychoanalysis.

Few, until Dianetics, had actually looked bluntly as they should at this problem and recognized to what extent the child . is the product of sex. The fact that there is a definite correlation between *children* and sex may appear to be a super-obvious statement. But how many people think babies are just too, too beautiful who, at the same time, feel that sex is just too, too nasty? The second dynamic must include not only sex and the sex act, but also children.

Perhaps the trend is to block the second dynamic so thoroughly that future generations will become completely insane. If this dwindling spiral of sexual aberration is not interrupted, there will be in the year 2000 or 2050, not 19,000,000 inmates in sanitariums and institutions, but a few sane people running for their lives from a country which is almost 100 percent insane.

A blocked second dynamic is accompanied by dislike of children, abuse of them and general impatience with them. It doesn't necessarily follow, however, that a blocked second dynamic is blocked both as to sex *and* children. It might be selectively blocked: open on sex and very thoroughly blocked on children, or wide open on children and thoroughly blocked on sex. When this latter condition is in evidence, the children resulting from such a union are very neurotic.[5]

It is evident, then, that the dwindling spiral winds up in the laps of the little kids. Children must bear the brunt of the results brought about by taboos which are the mores[6] of society. In order

5. **neurotic:** characterizing one who is insane or disturbed on some subject (as opposed to a psychotic person, who is just insane in general).

6. **mores:** folkways that are considered conducive to the welfare of society and so, through general observance, develop the force of law, often becoming part of the formal legal code.

to halt this spiral the most effective attack is the use of Preventive Dianetics,[7] as it applies to children and family life.

If a child can be prevented from acquiring engrams in the first place, the dwindling spiral is suddenly interrupted; and if those engrams latent in the reactive banks of children already born are prevented from keying-in, a seven-league step[8] is taken toward halting society's aberrational contagion.

To accomplish the first, society must shoulder some of the responsibility of taking adequate care of the mother. This is meant Dianetically rather than economically. Everyone must learn to say nothing within the expectant mother's hearing while she is hurt or ill, or during labor and delivery. Particularly during birth must absolute silence be maintained, and the more gentle the delivery, the better.

The finest birth, at first thought, would seem to be a Cesarean section,[9] since the child is believed to undergo none of the rigors of a normal birth. However, this is not the case. Cesarean births are harder on the child than ordinary birth because the obstetrician[10] usually waits until the child is very firmly wedged and indicates that it is not going to be born normally. The child is then left that way for about twelve or fourteen hours with his skull caved in.

---

7. **Preventive Dianetics:** that branch of Dianetics based on the principle that engrams can be held to minimal content or prevented entirely, with large gains in favor of mental health and physical well-being as well as social adjustment.

8. **seven-league step:** a step taken in seven-league boots, fairy-tale boots enabling the wearer to reach seven leagues at a stride. Figuratively, a *seven-league step* is significant forward progress.

9. **Cesarean section:** an operation by which a fetus is taken from the uterus by cutting through the walls of the abdomen and uterus.

10. **obstetrician:** a doctor who specializes in obstetrics, branch of medicine and surgery concerned with treating women before, in and after childbirth.

In one X-ray of a birth process the fetus' front bones were overlapped, the skull folded completely over on itself, because the mother's pelvic region was too small. The child remained in this condition for fourteen hours while people stood around having long conversations. The difference between the IQ of this boy and his brother, only a year older, is enormous. The young child is slow and clumsy, while his brother is sharp and alert. The older child was prematurely born and had a painless birth, so unexpected that the doctor didn't arrive in time. These children have almost identical prenatal engram banks. The big difference is birth.

Another case in point was a little girl who seemed to be only half awake when she was brought in for processing. She was very fat, and her normal physical development was badly retarded. Upon being asked what sort of delivery she had had, the mother said she guessed it was all right because she couldn't remember a thing about it. She had been unconscious for about twelve hours with chloroform.[11] Of course the child was anesthetized, too, through the umbilical cord. Doctors and nurses worked around the unconscious mother, talking, joking and laughing, charging both the mother's and the child's engram banks. Then the child was born. As far as the reactive mind time track is concerned, she remains right there at birth, sound asleep, in a continual dope-off.

Ordinarily a child's engrams do not start to key in until considerable time has elapsed. The necessity level is high, and he is in good shape generally. He could have a very heavily loaded engram bank, but it would take an extraordinary threat in environment to key in this material.

---

11. **chloroform:** a colorless liquid with a sharp, sweetish smell and taste. Chloroform evaporates quickly and easily. When its vapor is inhaled, it makes a person unconscious or unable to feel pain.

It is relatively difficult to tire children. They may appear to be tired but their level of "I'll quit and go to sleep" comes much later than in an adult. Only when a child is really pushed along and very badly tired out by some extraordinary circumstance does he reach a point where engramic material will key in.

It will be the first key-in that brings on the first sickness of the child. Although he is quite resilient and not easily injured, a hard bump which annoys him more than it pains him could cause a key-in for a few seconds afterwards. People normally take precautions to prevent accidents and anaten (a degree of attenuation of the analytical faculties) to children, so this does not have to be stressed. What does have to be stressed is the possibility of key-in at such times. There are engrams down in the bank which are matched in voice tone to the parents which can be all too easily keyed in. Hence, absolutely nothing should be said around the child right after injury of any kind. No matter how great the temptation to say, "Oh! You poor, dear little baby," let the kid howl. It is far better and safer to let minutes and minutes go by after an injury of any kind before you talk to the injured child, rather than risk key-in and restimulation.

Quarrels around a sleeping child are highly restimulative. The child is tired, goes to bed . . . and immediately the parents start quarreling. One case of stuttering originated in this manner. The child had been playing hours beyond his bedtime, having been out to an amusement park where the rides were so fascinating and everything so wonderful that he was too excited to sleep. He was even too tired to eat supper. He had been asleep only a half hour when his father came home intoxicated and a quarrel ensued. Some of the words used were "You can't talk to me like that!" and "Who do you think you're talking to?" The next morning when the child awakened he talked with a stutter—and he stuttered for the next twenty-two years.

Don't talk around a sick child. If the doctor decides to hold a long drawn-out conversation around the sickbed, your natural feeling of courtesy or awe might restrain you from doing something about it. But your natural feeling of courtesy or awe may help severely aberrate the child for the rest of his life. A good swift kick in the shin of anybody talking around a sick child, or—almost any physical violence would be justifiable under the circumstances. It sounds very strong, we know, but you can't help feeling punitive when you've been an auditor long enough to find all the aberrative talking that goes on around children. Even persons with the best of intentions can thoroughly ruin a child's life that way.

If punishment of a child becomes necessary, don't nag and hit the child and then nag some more. Tell the child the reason for the punishment in simple, direct language, and then apply the punishment *in absolute silence.* The punishment causes anaten; if talking goes on during and afterwards, the content of the lecture is grasped only on a *reactive* basis and becomes unavailable to the analytical mind. The child therefore cannot rationalize himself into good behavior. He analyzes only the fact that these people are horribly mean to him.

A child must always "honor his father and mother"—that's all there is to that! But nobody ever bothered to tell the child what parents have to do to be honored.

If a child is having a run of "accidentally" breaking things, interspersed with odds and ends of disobedience, it is almost a certainty that the child is being badly badgered from some quarter or other. The processing is not needed so much by the child as by the family, even though a family that has a very bad boy or very sick boy or girl may esteem[12] and comport[13]

12. **esteem:** hold to be; consider; regard.

13. **comport:** bear or conduct (themselves); behave.

themselves as veritable[14] saints of loving and understanding. They may never quarrel in the presence of the child. They may never unduly punish the child. The child may always have had the best of food and the best of care. But search the late-life bank of this child and see how many of these so-called "usual" childhood illnesses have been preceded by a very high emotional upset in the vicinity of that child!

In one family which was almost a model of propriety,[15] the little child had been very ill from a combination of chicken pox and pneumonia. A heavy quarrel had obviously taken place where the child slept, because the steel legs of the crib were bent from the weight of adult bodies falling against it. The beaverboard[16] wall was dented in the outline of adult knuckles or objects hurled in fury—yet this family supposedly lived a model life—they never quarreled around their child!

A four-year-old "bad" boy was taken to an auditor. According to the parents, if he had been six feet tall he would have given Genghis Khan[17] a good run for his money. He would go upstairs and pull Mama's clothes off the hangers and practice mutilation on them with scissors. He would go into another room, preferably one which was very neat and tidy, and slash the wallpaper with a knife. Someone in the family about to eat breakfast would find his cereal liberally sprinkled with shredded cigarettes. He was artfully clumsy; he seemed able to break selectively every valuable piece of bric-a-brac in the house.

---

14. **veritable:** having all the qualities or attributes of the specified person or thing.

15. **propriety:** conformity to established standards of good or proper behavior or manners.

16. **beaverboard:** a light, stiff sheeting made of wood fiber and used in building, especially for partitions or temporary structures.

17. **Genghis Khan:** (1162–1227) Mongol conqueror of most of Asia and of east Europe to the Dnieper River.

What he obviously needed, they said, was more discipline. Inquiry into how much discipline he had experienced brought out chastisement averaging four spankings and a clout on the head a day. The only thing that could be said for the punishment was that it was consistent: no matter what happened, he was punished. Furthermore, there was unanimity[18] in the family. Father agreed and punished him. Mother agreed and punished him. And the one grandparent who was always around also agreed and punished him. Here was a red-hot rebel, a veritable insurgent[19] in the community, leading a successful revolt.

The matter was solved very simply. The auditor, taking note of the fact that the adults who brought the boy were not very tall, made the announcement that the next person who laid a hand on the child would be personally accountable to him. They agreed that this was a new reality, and within twenty-four hours there was a change in the young preclear. He picked up his own clothes. He began to do the dishes! Suddenly he was no longer a hellion.[20]

It is absolutely wonderful to watch children who have not been "disciplined." They are not any the worse for it. If you want to see a really, thoroughly wicked kid, find one that's had a big dose of discipline. He knows exactly what he's supposed to do, and so long as he's got breath in his body, he's doggone if he'll do it! He is confronted by a society that is shot through with a blocked second dynamic as a fashionable thing. He is confronted with people who don't like children and who apply to him all manner of barbarism on the excuse that this promotes loyalty and discipline.

---

18. **unanimity:** complete accord or agreement; being unanimous.
19. **insurgent:** a person who rises in revolt; rebel.
20. **hellion:** a disorderly, troublesome, rowdy or mischievous person.

There are two particularly insidious[21] lines in society with regard to children. One is the belief that parenthood is a biological fact but that the child has no natural affection for the parents and could be raised just as well by anybody else. The other is one which teaches the child not to grow up because (1) it pays a high bonus to be a child, and (2) grown-ups don't have any fun, so why be a grown-up?

There is an obvious natural affection of the child for his own particular parents and, despite theories to the contrary, a child gets along much better with his own parents. Actually the parents' voices are frequently restimulative, making all manner of things wrong with the relationship on a reactive level, but the child usually has enough affinity and affection for his own parents to overcome the bulk of this.

An auditor received a phone call one day from a gentleman who said, "I don't know what could possibly be wrong with my daughter. She has run away from home three times." Questioning revealed that he had always been very careful never to demonstrate any affection for her, for fear of setting up some complex[22] or other, he said, and that she had often complained of having "no family life worth sticking around for." This man had been careful all his life not to be affectionate; he thought children could be spoiled by loving them. The way to spoil children is by *not* loving them.

No child was ever spoiled by affection, by sympathy, by kindness, by understanding or even by indulgence. The old

---

21. **insidious:** operating or proceeding in an inconspicuous or seemingly harmless way but actually with grave effect.

22. **complex:** *(psychology)* an idea or group of repressed ideas associated with a past emotional disturbance so as to influence a person's present behavior to a great or excessive degree.

---

superstition that love and affection so thoroughly upset a child that they drive him crazy is incredible. A child can have better toys than anybody on the block and it won't make a snob out of him. If he is permitted to grow in the society of children, he will make an adequate analysis concerning his possessions, and instinctively share them. He will find out for himself how to make the best out of life.

The reverse of this is that most of the children in our society today are denied any responsibility or position of any kind. From his first breath the child begins to be denied the independence which every organism seeks. He is fitted into a sort of mold which is supposedly desirable or "best for him," cutting off his freedom of action and expression in all directions. Fortunately for him, he has at least one goal—to grow up. He might have other necessary goals, but they are minor compared to this one saving grace;[23] he can salvage himself on that alone—that is, unless he is carefully taught *not* to grow up.

If he decides that growing up is something that will result in a bad state of affairs for him, that the desirable thing is to remain a child, he has been robbed of the one goal which, despite antagonistic influences, would carry him forward. Children who have received too large a bonus for being children are those who progress the least satisfactorily.

A modern school of thought, one of the very many, gives to children a position in the home which far exceeds their actual state. The youngster is assigned an importance of being a child that is vastly out of proportion to the importance of being an adult. If little Willie suddenly runs into a room, knocks over the lamp and spills some sticky pineapple juice on a guest's suit,

---

23. **saving grace:** a quality that makes up for other generally negative characteristics; redeeming feature.

that's all right. Pat little Willie on the head and give him some more pineapple juice. Tell the guest that "He's only a little child and doesn't know any better." This kind of training for children places a very high priority on remaining a child. Actually, who would want to be an adult in such a family?

How does the child determine whether growing up is desirable? He has enormous energy and good repair and healing qualities. He is naturally very energetic and active. He has, as a general rule, a pretty good mind, so he looks around one day and says to himself, "Now, let's see. I'm growing up. What will I be when I grow up? I will be an adult, of course." Then he begins to observe very closely the adults in his immediate neighborhood, beginning with the family.

Here's Mama, whose full concentration is on being a waiting maid to children. He doesn't want to be Mama—she doesn't have any fun. There's Papa. He drags home from work, manages a smile, and maybe gets a chance to look at the paper before he tiredly eats dinner and goes to bed. And then he complains about the kids making too much noise. The child perforce concludes, "He isn't very elegant, either." After a brief scan of the lesser relatives, he begins to scratch his head and wonders, "What the heck is this grown-up business? I want to stay a kid, 'cause look—we get waited on, get food, clothing, 'n everything."

If you can detach yourself from your present attitude on "reality" and take a truly objective look at it, you will see it from a viewpoint very much like that of a child. The child knows that he likes to run and play, and has an idea that other people ought to like to run and play, too. A large section of adult society believes that running and playing is very wicked indeed. It's just not done. At least, most grown-ups don't do it. They *never* have much fun.

The child, fortunately, has a very high sense of reality, but has been completely surrounded by adult delusions. He isn't running on the kind of reality on which everyone is agreed, but the one which he sees and interprets according to *his* data. It is no delusion to him.

He agrees perfectly that he is Hopalong Cassidy[24] between the hours of four and six, and that somebody else is Little Beaver[25] during the same hours. There is no lack of agreement and no lack of reality; his is the greater reality simply because he can face it on the whole periphery[26] as well as narrow it down to selective reality. The mechanism in him which sets up his sense of reality is far more vivid and unrestricted than that of an adult, who after all must submit to the kind of reality which clamps him to a desk or workbench.

Work, economic servitude, whether he likes it or not, is the adult's reality—but what a poor substitute! It is the super-artificiality on which he has to agree figuratively at the point of a gun. Society has said, "If you don't consider your job the greatest reality in your life, the only one, we're going to starve you, Bud." So he grudgingly agrees. Reality? No! It's an agreed-upon stratum of society, an agreed-upon code of action.

The child is also very sensitive to unreality. If someone, talking from the point of view of his own narrow sense of reality, tries to tell him the reason why such and such takes place, the child is likely to stare rather blankly, unable to figure it all out. He will have to be told many times over. He has to be told in grade

---

24. **Hopalong Cassidy:** a cowboy hero in a series of western movies made in the 1930s.

25. **Little Beaver:** the name of a Navaho orphan adopted by a cowboy named Red Rider, characters in a nationally syndicated comic strip by Fred Harmon. Little Beaver became a radio show in 1942.

26. **periphery:** surrounding space or area; outer parts; environs or outskirts.

school, high school, college, and then when he gets married and is told by the boss, he finally gets the idea. Suddenly he agrees that the thing he's been told all his life is indeed a reality. At that moment he begins to fold up.

One of the best ways to put children on a happy road is by offering them a little education. Interest them in the real world, and try to interest them in a hobby in which they can learn to use their bodies. Let them choose the hobby, and let them show how proficient they can become. Teach them walking tightropes or how to fry eggs. The world isn't a bunch of selected subjects that somebody writes down in a book. This is the business of living, and if something is especially interesting to the child, that's the thing to teach. If a precision control of the child's body can be built up, it will aid his sanity, raise his tone, and make his processing easier.

Just plain learning a skill isn't good enough, because the farther that skill departs from practical application in the future, the less efficacy[27] it will have in straightening out his mental and physical health. The child must see that what he is learning leads toward an actual need in his life. Give the child a feeling of pride in himself, and a feeling of independence about some certain thing. It is absolutely necessary that Johnny have reserved to him alone at least one sphere of action in which he is completely independent.

A little boy walking downtown with his parents saw an accordion in a window and suddenly decided that he wanted to learn to play the accordion. After a session of whining and screaming he acquired a small accordion and, despite the cartoons, finally learned to play something. "I always thought it was a good idea to start him on the accordion," they gloated, one

---

27. **efficacy:** capacity for producing a desired result or effect; effectiveness.

after the other. They fought among themselves for the distinction of being the first to recognize genius. Then they lowered the boom.

"You must practice an hour and seventeen minutes every day, like it says in the book. You're not going to go out and play with that gang of rowdies." It was no longer the child's accordion and no longer his music. One day the accordion just "happened" to get smashed. The parents made their excuses—"You know how children are, they're flighty and changeable. They don't know what they want next."

The child had selected something he wanted to do. When he found it was not an independent sphere of action, he abandoned it.

A child can be robbed of independence of action in numerous ways. Preventing him from making his own decisions by inflicting punishment upon him when his own decisions lead him into trouble is one way. Another is to try continually to impress him with how nice everybody is to him, and how the world is all run for him, and how ungrateful he is. Another way, a particularly despicable and demoralizing way, is to work on his sympathy by getting sick, or tired, or discouraged when he does anything wrong.

Have you ever seen a mother who handled a child with a tyranny presumably subtler but actually far more destructive than that of a Roman emperor, simply by bringing home to the child that all of poor "Mama's" travail and all of "Mama's" sickness and weariness is because "Mama" gives *her all* for the child? It is too, too patent[28] that the child is expected to do a little something in return; at least, if the "child" is a grown-up girl, to

---

28. **patent:** readily open to notice or observation; evident; obvious.

be a little bit obedient and—not marry John. The pitiful aspect of the situation is that if the young girl does cut loose from her moorings and marries John, something usually does happen to "Mama," who goes ahead and finishes the dramatization.

The child who is chronically afraid is usually in a widely scattered state of mind. His standard banks do not have enough data to permit him to select what is wrong and identify it. It is a wide, unknown world to him because parts and portions of it are not identified; hence the extreme terror. The world of the child is one of giants and dragons, not because all childhood is delusion, but simply because children do not have enough data.

One particular poem is responsible for more upsets in children than any other piece of work. Something to the effect that "Daddy heard him holler and Mama heard him shout, but when they went upstairs there was nothing left but a pile of clothes. The goblins[29] had gotten him!" "What's a goblin, Mama?" "That's someone that eats little children." Childhood delusion? Grown-up delusion is more to the point!

It is absolutely unnecessary to communicate with a child on this level. A child is perfectly logical. There is no sense in telling him that goblins exist and that there is a place called hell where he will burn forever, and that the soul inside him is going to be taken by the Lord, who doesn't exist as far as his own data and reality are concerned. Sir James Jeans[30] and many others have been trying for a long time to identify just what the soul is and have not succeeded even to their own satisfaction; and yet this little child, two or three or four years old, is expected to say devoutly, "The Lord . . . going to come when I'm asleep. . . . "

29. **goblins:** grotesque sprites or elves that are mischievous or malicious toward people.

30. **Sir James Jeans:** (1877–1946) English astrophysicist and author.

He will parrot it, yes, but it will threaten and frighten him more than it will be logical to him.

Perhaps the most insidious thing that can happen to the child is the exterior ally. Until you have processed a number of people you may not realize how deadly is the ally in the sympathy engram. Grandparents should not be permitted into the home of their grandchildren until they have learned to behave themselves Dianetically. One can have all the mawkish[31] sentimentality in the world and think, "My dear, dear grandparents"—but wait until you get back there in the reactive bank and find out what they did. They were very *nice*, true, but all too often they bought the child off and broke the affinity line between the parents and the child.

A grandmother stepping in and undermining the situation until she is receiving the affection from the child which belongs to the parents, has actually had to do just that. She demonstrates to the child that the parents are cruel, by reviling[32] Mama each time Mama corrects the child, thus setting herself up during moments of pain and anguish as an ally. Any family that permits to exist within it people who split up this natural affinity between children and parents is asking for future trouble with the child's mental condition.

An ally blurting out to a feverish child, "My dear, I'm going to stay here until you are well," becomes a leech upon that child's mind. Consider what happens when a child gets very ill and Grandma rants, "Do you think he will die? Oh, my dear, darling little baby, you are going to die. I know you are going to die. Please don't leave me!"

---

31. **mawkish:** characterized by a sickly sentimentality; weakly emotional; maudlin.
32. **reviling:** calling bad names; abusing with words.

Later on in life the child slides into Grandma's valence, and a period of illness which originally ran about five days is keyed in and keeps the child sick for months!

Working with children will be at once a fascinating and arduous adventure. The auditor who applies insight and patience along with his skill will be rewarded by seeing children progress from little rebels and urchins,[33] from sickly unawareness and misery, to cooperative, healthy members of society. He will find it necessary to face the inconsistency of parents as well as children. The task will seem impossible and heartbreaking at times, but in the end there will be an unequalled sense of accomplishment, of having done something really worthwhile for the advancement of future generations.

---

33. **urchins:** mischievous boys.

4

Standard Dianetic Technique

4

Standard Dianetic Technique

In discussing Dianetics as applied to the special problems of children, frequent reference is made to a compilation of techniques known as Standard Procedure. With the knowledge of the existence of an engram in mind, it was necessary to devise a method for contacting and reducing or erasing that engram. The method had to give uniform results, and had to work in all cases. This method, when formulated and codified, became known as Standard Procedure.

Since, in the best interests of a child, it is often necessary to process one or more adults within the immediate environment, a brief outlining of the steps involved in Standard Procedure may be helpful. The outgrowth of this technique as applicable to children will be found in later chapters.

How seldom in this busy modern life we find anyone who is genuinely interested in our problems, our fears and our dislikes. Time and time again we hopefully begin a conversation with the deep-down purpose of getting something off our chest, but as often does our listener interject with problems of his own; "Oh, that reminds me of the time . . ." And suddenly our little troubles are as nothing compared to his soul-shattering and earth-trembling disappointments. Instead of getting something off our chests we have become the listener, the auditor. We sigh, bury our disappointment in a wan[1] smile and listen. It is a strange truth that the best listener is often he who most needs a sympathetic listener.

Thus is affinity established. When you begin to audit a member of your family, a friend or relative, ask him many questions about things in present time—how he feels about current questions of the day, how he agrees or disagrees with people around him. Sound him out on his methods of communication to others, and as to how he receives communication, but do not in any way disagree with him! People have disagreed with him all his life. It is not for a Dianetic auditor to add himself to an already over-subscribed list.

Affinity between the auditor and preclear is of utmost importance. The preclear must have confidence in the auditor, both as to his integrity as a person, and as to his ability as an auditor to handle anything which may come up during a session. Communication between auditor and preclear must be of such nature as to preclude reservation. The reality of any auditing session will greatly depend upon observance of these two factors.

Having established some basis for present time enjoyment, beliefs and hopes in your preclear, direct his attention to those items or individuals within his environ[2] having a high reality value for him. The person he *knows* is his friend, the stone stairs leading to the front door that he is absolutely certain are real, and the children which he sired and feels are truly *his* children— all of these and many more make for an increase in the present

1. **wan:** showing or suggesting ill health, fatigue, unhappiness, etc.
2. **environ:** abbreviation for environment.

time affinity with life of the preclear. It is up to you, the auditor, to question the preclear in such a way that he contacts moments in which these things are real.

The items so far delineated are your means of evaluating your preclear. You are finding out by questions, by discussion and by listening to what he has to say roughly where your preclear lies on an arbitrary scale from the highest possible sanity to the lowest depths of insanity and death. The methods you use to process the preclear from this point on will depend upon your evaluation. Obviously, for those lying very low on the scale (termed in Dianetics the Tone Scale[3]), very light methods must be used. It is definitely not recommended that the inexperienced auditor attempt to process someone who is violently insane, or even apathetically insane. But above the lower levels of the Tone Scale a preclear may be accepted with confidence that you can, by using Dianetic techniques, increase the happiness and well-being of a child's father or mother, and thereby reduce the difficulties of the child in familial relations.

A record of each session should be kept. There is no need for it to be a *verbatim* account of every word, motion or flick of an eyelid of the preclear, but pertinent facts should be noted. Write down the age, the number of brothers and sisters of the preclear, and whether any of his immediate family has died. Record his "pet" phrases for future check against primary or secondary[4] engram content.

---

3. **Tone Scale:** a scale which shows the emotional tones of a person. These, ranged from the highest to the lowest, are, in part, serenity, enthusiasm (as we proceed downward), conservatism, boredom, antagonism, anger, covert hostility, fear, grief, apathy.

4. **secondary:** a period of anguish brought about by a major loss or threat of loss to the individual. The secondary engram depends for its strength and force upon physical-pain engrams which underlie it.

After you have made a preliminary scouting of the case, begin to use Straightwire⁵ (straight line memory) to any recollections of any kind in the preclear's life. Ask him about childhood moments of happiness, when he graduated from school, and when he had a teacher he especially liked. Orient your preclear's past for him in this manner until actual existence of a past is established in your preclear's reality. It may be surprising to find many people whose pasts are a jumble of complete unreality, in which they are uncertain that anything actually happened to them. Straightwire will assist the preclear to increase the reality of his past, which is, in effect, straightening out a portion of his time track.

To gain this much in your preclear's case you may have spent two hours, or even three weeks or more of daily sessions.

When the preclear has established a few definite "guideposts" in his past—moments when his affinity and reality were very high—it is then time to seek out a very light lock chain⁶ by questioning. Note the incidents on paper as they are found. And then when the chain seems to be complete, to have no additional incidents of a similar nature to contact, question the preclear again on the same incidents, one by one in the same order as they appeared the first time.

Then do the same thing again, using only those incidents

---

5. **Straightwire:** the name of a process. It is the act of stringing a line between present time and some incident in the past, and stringing that line directly and without any detours. The auditor is stringing a straight "wire" of memory between the actual genus (origin) of a condition and present time, thus demonstrating that there is a difference of time and space in the condition then and the condition now, and that the preclear, conceding this difference, then rids himself of the condition or at least is able to handle it.

6. **chain:** a succession of incidents, occurring at various intervals along the time track, that are related to one another by some similarity of either subject, general location, people or perception. Such a succession of similar incidents may span a brief period or a very long period of time.

contacted, unless the preclear insists upon adding new ones of a similar nature. Continue asking questions selectively about these specific incidents in their proper order until the preclear has obviously raised in tone. This technique is known to Hubbard Dianetic Auditors as "Repetitive Straightwire."[7]

During such running of analytical moments, the preclear will almost surely attempt to contact moments of anger, grief, fear or anaten. Keep him on the original subject by addressing your questions only to the analytical moments on the chain. And do not be surprised if the preclear "dopes off." This is a condition wherein the preclear apparently goes sound asleep, sometimes snoring loudly, sometimes mumbling, and other times merely lying quietly saying nothing. During these periods, which may extend any length of time from one minute to eight hours or longer, do not disturb your preclear by questions. Sit alertly by, and wait for him to come up out of the dope-off.

This condition is caused by unconsciousness in the preclear's past. Dope-off seems to be the present time discharge of past unconsciousness. It is particularly noticeable and heavy on a case which was the recipient of a number of attempted abortions performed while he was in the womb. After a short or extended period of dope-off the preclear will have a noticeable rise of tone in present time. He will be more alert, more interested in the world around him. This may well be the first major sign of improvement in your preclear.

You may have a preclear whose perceptics, i.e., his perception of sound, time and motion, visio, etc., are all on full. If not, continue processing as you have been until his tone rises and his

---

7. **Repetitive Straightwire:** attention called to an incident over and over amongst other incidents until it is desensitized. Used on conclusions or incidents which do not easily surrender.

perceptions turn on and he has a high sense of reality about both the past and present time.

When he fits the latter description you may then begin to work with his "file clerk." The file clerk is his "basic personality." Just as its name implies, the file clerk answers a question directed to the preclear, by giving dates, time, ages, yes or no answers and, in fact, any desired datum concerning the file of memory data in the preclear's mind. To initiate the action of the file clerk, instruct the preclear to give the first word or phrase which flashes into his mind as you ask him a certain question. For instance:

"Answer yes or no—is there a chain of locks available now?"

"Yes!"

"What is the name of this chain?"

"Whipping."

In this way an auditor prepares his ground for the work of a particular session.

In another section of this book there is mentioned an "age flash." This is simply a file clerk answer to the question, "How old are you?" or "What is your age?" or just the single word (after the file clerk has become very reliable) "Age?" It will surprise you, if you are a beginning auditor, how many people will answer seemingly ridiculous numbers when asked for an age flash. It is interesting to try on various friends. Merely instruct them to give the first number which occurs to them after you ask the question, "What is your age?"

But the numbers are seldom ridiculous. Suppose a preclear

whom you know to be thirty-six years old gives an age flash of thirteen. She is flustered and cannot understand why she gave such a silly number—but then question her about an incident at the age of thirteen. Better still, use the file clerk for a few moments longer to establish the geography of the incident:

"Please answer yes or no: Hospital?"

"Yes."

"Doctor?"

"No!"

"Nurse?"

"Yes."

In this manner the nature and locale of the incident which has caused the preclear to be stuck on the time track is determined. Occasionally the number given by the preclear is not a measure of years, but of days or months postnatal. The time of reference can be established easily by asking the file clerk (after an answer of eight, for instance):

"Days?"

"No."

"Weeks?"

"Yes!"

The mechanism of the file clerk is such that, when validated by acceptance of its answers, it gives correct information concerning events, time and directions for proceeding with the case.

A file clerk, when asked for the incident next needed to resolve the case, will give an answer which will be either a clue or a direct delineation of what should come next.

Invalidation of the file clerk is tantamount[8] to stalling the case. A file clerk can be invalidated by inferred or direct disbelief in the correctness of the answers given.

When you have worked with the file clerk for a time and have established to your own satisfaction that it is giving valid answers to your questions (sometimes a file clerk's answers are filtered through a heavy "circuit" and are not valid, but even so, the auditor must not allow the basic personality of his preclear to suspect that he does not believe the answers) ask for the earliest moment of pain or unconsciousness necessary to resolve the case. This is a suggested routine:

"The file clerk will give the earliest moment of pain or unconsciousness necessary to resolve the case. The 'somatic strip'[9] will go to this incident."

The somatic strip is another mechanism, but one which is commanded in no uncertain terms. Where the file clerk is asked for an incident, the somatic strip is commanded. The somatic strip might be likened to the pickup[10] on a phonograph, except

---

8. **tantamount:** equivalent, as in value, force, effect or signification.

9. **somatic strip:** a physical indicator mechanism which has to do with time. The auditor orders the somatic strip. The somatic strip can be sent back to the beginning of an engram and will go there. The somatic strip will advance through an engram in terms of minutes counted off by the auditor, so that the auditor can say that the somatic strip will go to the beginning of the engram, then to the point five minutes after the engram began, and so forth.

10. **pickup:** a small device attached to the end of a phonograph tone arm that contains a stylus and the mechanism that translates the movement of the stylus in a record groove into a changing electrical voltage.

that it would have many needles representing the various perceptics instead of only one. The phonograph pickup may be placed at any point on a recording and the sound track will play off whatever is recorded, from that point. The somatic strip is commanded to go to the various points on the preclear's time track, and it goes there. It will obey the command to go forward through the incident which the file clerk has handed out. Part of the "I" of the preclear will then perceive in recall those things which happened at any time in his life, from a few hours before conception to present time. When you command a preclear to "come up to present time," you have commanded the somatic strip to leave an incident (which some never do until that incident—if aberrative—is reduced or erased by many repetitions).

Suppose you have ordered the somatic strip of your preclear to contact an incident, and conversation appears to the preclear. Have him repeat the phrases which he hears, but in addition, coax him to feel the other perceptics as well. Chances are, if it is a painful incident he has contacted, he will be feeling the somatics (pain) of the incident without your invitation. For the beginning auditor, this is the moment when he needs courage and confidence in his tools. When the preclear is apparently in the most intense pain, his eyes burning perhaps, you must calmly continue to run the incident, asking for any phrases connected with the incident, and picking up all sounds, sense of touch and kinesthesia[11] as they appear. The somatic strip will play back whatever was recorded. And then, when the incident seems to be over and the pain has subsided, command the somatic strip to go to the beginning of the incident and roll it again! Do this several times, until the preclear goes through the cycle of apathy,

---

11. **kinesthesia:** the sensation of position, movement, tension, etc., of parts of the body.

anger, boredom and after perhaps the eighth time through the incident, is cheerful and perhaps even heartily laughing about the whole thing. Pay no attention to any efforts he may make to avoid going through a second or third time. If you accede to his demand to change the subject, or to go on to something else, you will bog down the case and give the preclear some very, very uncomfortable present time somatics.

If you have run an engram, and feel that you have spent sufficient time in session for the day, direct your preclear to pick up a moment of pleasure which occurred sometime during his life, and run that through exactly as though it were an engram, three or four times. Then command the preclear to "come up to present time."

If, when you first commanded the somatic strip to contact the engram handed out by the file clerk, your preclear did not contact the incident, it may be necessary to run some secondaries which are sitting on top of the engram. A secondary is a late-life incident containing painful emotion which activated the engram. It may be the loss of a pet, the death of a member of the family or the loss of an ally. Carefully question the preclear to find whatever might be available and then run the incident from the moment of awareness of loss to the point where the analyzer has resumed operation. Then the preclear is returned to the beginning of the incident and it is run again, exactly as though it were a basic engram. With successive passes through the incident, the preclear will rise through grief, anger, boredom and finally, cheerfulness. It seems strange, perhaps, that anyone could be cheerful about the death of his mother, but when the grief secondary—one of the most aberrative occurrences in an individual's life—has been run to erasure, cheerfulness will be in evidence.

After running a secondary you will notice a distinct rise in the general tone of the preclear in his everyday pursuits. It will be gratifying to find that he no longer slaps the children for every breach of what he might term "discipline." He has been raised on the Tone Scale, and an aberrative portion of his past life has been eliminated from his reactive mind.

But there are dozens, sometimes hundreds, of secondaries in everyone's life. As many of these as possible should be run. When they no longer present themselves, when the preclear can find no other incident containing painful emotion, return the preclear to the prenatal area by asking the file clerk for the earliest available incident needed to resolve the case and command the somatic strip (or the preclear) to go to the beginning of the incident. Run the engram presented, and then, after no additional engrams are available, ask once again for new secondaries which may, by this time, be available.

During the final moments of each session with your preclear, Straightwire him on everything which occurred during the session including anything you might have done to irritate him. Ask him what happened when you began, what came up first, what the engram (if any) was like. Ask him if he heard any voices within the room or without. Make certain that he has firmly in mind everything that occurred during the session, because only then can you feel sure that whatever he has run is fixed firmly in the analytical mind. End each session with a brief pleasure moment. Let him pick the pleasure moment, and run it through two or three times, and then bring him up to present time.

This is the basis of Standard Procedure. There are refinements of course. A professional auditor who has been trained by the Foundation* is familiar with many techniques which fit special conditions. It is not expected that one become an expert auditor from the techniques as outlined here, but, if a preclear is chosen with care so as not to accept a person who is extremely low on the Tone Scale, there is no reason why any intelligent adult could not put the techniques into practice and expect to obtain gratifying results.

One last word of caution: These techniques, as outlined in this chapter, are techniques for use on adults or children in their teens. For younger children there are variations on this procedure.

* Dianetics auditor training is available in the Hubbard Dianetics Foundation Department of Churches of Scientology. Professional auditor training is also available in Church of Scientology Academies. For the address of the organization nearest you, see the address list at the back of this book. —Editor

5

Dianetic Processing for Children

5

Dianetic Processing for Children

It is possible to process a child at any age level beyond the point when he learns to speak. However, no serious processing should be undertaken until the child is at least five. Extensive Dianetic processing is not encouraged, except in very unusual circumstances, until the child is at least eight years of age. Much good can be accomplished before the age of eight by straight line memory technique, and in the period from eight to twelve years the child may be processed by any of the techniques outlined here. But one should not force the child into the prenatal area until he is at least twelve years old. If a return to the basic area is made by the child, it is to be accepted and treated as a matter of course and engrams reduced or erased, but the auditor should not in any way force the child to do so.

In all except severe cases, a child may be successfully processed by a parent. In all cases, however, it is more difficult for a parent than for an outside auditor, since the parent, by virtue of being the causative agent, is a restimulator for the child. The very tone of a parent's voice, even without similarity of word content, will sometimes act as a restimulator. Nevertheless, with some intelligence and objectivity on the part of the parent, it can be done. It should be set up as a well-defined program occurring in a form differing appreciably from any other household happening or chore. It should be handled as a new, exciting game in which the rules are slightly different from those of other forms of play. Even if the processing is done by an auditor from outside the household, the parents still form an essential part of the child's environment and must be educated into an acceptance of the vital facts and values of Dianetics.

There are three major steps in the processing of children:

1. Prevent restimulation.

2. Break locks.

3. Deintensify painful emotion.

The parent should try to avoid the language which is in the child's reactive bank. The emotions accompanying this language should also be avoided, as well as any known duplication of situations which are likely to have been recorded by the child's reactive mind. If the parent cannot recall the incidents in which engrams might have been created, or if she cannot remember the language used at that time, she can soon determine by the child's reactions what sets of words and what kinds of emotion are in the child's reactive bank. She should then be very careful to avoid this language, especially when situations exist which might be engramic. Any aberration in a child is evidence that a key-in has occurred, and the situations in which the aberrations are most apparent will have perceptions similar to the perceptics which were present when the engram was laid in.

For example, one set of parents tried desperately to keep their child from wetting the bed by continually telling him to go to bed and not to drink any water before retiring. In spite of this "education," the child continued to wet the bed. Dianetic evaluation of the situation revealed immediately that something in the child's environment was restimulating an engramic command which caused the bed-wetting. In this case, as in many others, the action taken in good faith by the Dianetically untrained parents was not preventing the aberration but, rather, keeping it chronically keyed in. These parents found that commands which meant reactively that if you mention the word *water* you must urinate in bed, were contained in the birth engram. The actual engram content was:

"The water is going to come."

"It'll break and go in the bed."

"Just lie there and let it go."

The engram was deactivated when the restimulators were removed. When the parents stopped mentioning the word *water* before the child went to bed, the bed-wetting tapered off and then stopped entirely.

Locks can be contacted and blown through straight line memory techniques; that is, without reverie.[1] The parent can be of great help in this part of the process because she knows pretty well when she has created a lock, especially in an emotional blow-up of any kind. By remembering the standard pattern of her dramatizations during emotional crises, she can help the child or the child's auditor to find the locks which will best help the child to overcome his difficulties. Whenever anaten is present in the child, and it is present when any engram is being restimulated, a lock can be erected. The resulting aberration will depend on the emotion and pain of the lock as well as on the original engram.

---

1. **reverie:** a light state of "concentration" which the preclear is placed in, not to be confused with hypnosis; in reverie the person is fully aware of what is taking place.

This fact, plus the nature of the aberration, can be used to determine which locks should be investigated first.

In a child, returning is a simple and natural mechanism, and the technique of blowing locks is to use a combination of memory and recall. Ask the child, for instance, if his mother ever bawled him out. If so, try to get him to remember a specific incident. At this point many children will close their eyes and return to the event. If the child can remember the exact words his mother used, and the words of any other persons in the incident, allow him to run through the incident as often as it interests him. Most locks will blow with a single recounting, and will cease to have any aberrative effect on the child.

Grief can be contacted in a child as easily as in an adult. The chief point of difference is that the grief will be on moments which seem not very important to an adult. A child will have a definite sense of loss when, for example, his mother did not allow him to sail his boat on a rainy day. The discharge over this type of grief engram will be small when compared to the grief occasioned by the leaving of a favorite nurse or the loss of a pet, but any moment of grief which can be discharged will improve the health and well-being of the child.

The auditor who wishes to deal successfully with children must have, above all, the ability to establish affinity with the child. This is a problem of interesting the child in the incidents which have caused his difficulty. A child's attention is badly scattered. He has not yet learned to focus his attention well, and it is the function of the auditor to pick up his attention and channel it back against the locks and grief engrams.

A child has a great natural sense of dignity. Do not talk down to him. Treat him with as much dignity as you can. You will find that the child has weird misconceptions about many everyday things around him. Trace these misconceptions to their source and you will usually find an adult who has not taken the trouble to give this child the right data. *Never talk over a child's head to his parents.* It is better to talk over the heads of the parents to the child, always working with him on a partnership basis.

Quite often the processing of a child inevitably involves more than working with the child alone. Much of the aberration found in him will have come from a lack of Dianetic knowledge on the part of the parents, and steps other than putting the child on a couch and removing locks and running grief engrams need to be taken in the interest of preventing restimulation.

There are three ways of treating a person Dianetically, and all of them are sometimes necessary in the processing of a child:

1.   Standard processing procedures.

2.   Dianetic education.

3.   Shifting environment.

You can usually count on the parents being very anxious to have their children better and healthier. You can also count on the fact, unfortunately, that the parents are going to take your advice only to a very limited degree. It may be up to you to enforce in some manner those items which you advance as the parents' duty toward the child.

One little boy who wouldn't talk at all was brought to an auditor. After many fruitless attempts to gain a case opening, the auditor asked the boy which of his parents had told him he would be punished if he said anything about their quarrels. Tears! A rush of words. Case opening!

How is an auditor to do something for a child if the parents forbid him to tell anything about his home life? These parents were certain that reading comic books was responsible for the child's aberration, but during the entire course of their marital "misnavigation off the middle of the hurricane section" they quite customarily fought at every meal. Father would start complaining about the food, and Mother would complain how hard she had to work. It was not unusual for them to pick up the crockery and shy[2] it at each other, and not extraordinary for the boy to be hit. He could not be induced to eat and though the average weight for a boy of his age was eighty-five pounds, he barely tipped the scales at fifty-eight.

The prescription in this case was merely straight line memory technique on the first time his parents quarreled at the table in his presence. The next thing was to insist that the child be permitted to eat in the kitchen behind closed doors.

When they heard this, both parents looked daggers at the child and said, "What have you been telling him?" The auditor could see the child was probably in for a beating, so he warned the parents: "I know that if this boy is allowed to eat by himself he will gain weight; if in the next couple of weeks this child does *not* gain weight, I'll have to call the humane society."[3]

The child gained weight.

The auditor who deals with children needs to evaluate the child's environment from a Dianetic standpoint. In many cases it will be the parents who need processing most, not the child. In any case, it is important that the parents understand what key-ins are, and how to avoid them. One of the important points

2. **shy:** throw with a swift, sudden movement.

3. **humane society:** a group of persons organized to protect children or animals from cruelty.

to remember in this connection is that the "usual" childhood illnesses quite often occur *three days after* some emotional upset in the home. In processing the child, make sure to explore the area which preceded any illness he may have had. The chances of finding the key-in which helped to bring it on are excellent. The first sickness of the child will help you locate the first key-in. If enough of these are found in the child, the parents will be convinced of the necessity of preventing further key-ins. If the child's processing does not provide enough evidence to persuade the parents of the importance of key-ins on the health of the child, it is the duty of the auditor processing the child to demonstrate on one of the parents that such key-ins do take place, and that key-ins do affect an individual's health and happiness, young or old.

A small amount of education for the parents in the principles of Child Dianetics will sometimes accomplish more than the same number of hours spent in processing the child. Perhaps the most important single point in such education is to make clear to the parents the urgent necessity of giving goals to a child, and the most vital goal is that of growing up to be an adult. A child should have responsibility and independence commensurate with his status as a child. He should have things which are wholly his, and about which he decides everything. But under no circumstances should he be possessed automatically of as much right as an adult in the sphere of the home. To give him such privileges prematurely is to remove the main goal of his life: growing up. The child, cared for without question and trained toward nothing, loses his prime incentive in life, especially when he sees the adults around him who do not enjoy themselves as adults, take no pleasure in their rights as adults, and do not insist on their rights as adults. When a child is kept dependent and shielded and recompensed for being a child, his incentive for being otherwise is much reduced, with a consequent deterioration of ability to acquire knowledge and a serious reduction in the quantity he will acquire, since he does not see any reason in acquiring it.

Education of the parents includes, of course, the basic ideas of Preventive Dianetics. Don't talk around a sick or injured child. As soon as anaten begins to depart after a minor accident, act to make the child comfortable, but for several minutes thereafter do not talk. Don't leave the child in a restimulative atmosphere. Don't take a child up from the middle of a nice sleep and tell her repeatedly to "Sit there in that chair and listen to what a terrible thing it is to be married to a man," as one mother did. Try and keep the child away from highly charged dramatizations of any kind. Care for the child efficiently and quietly, but do not establish yourself as an indispensable ally.

If an auditor finds at the beginning of processing that the child he is working with is in need of constructive things to do (and this will be customary rather than unusual), it is sometimes a good thing to set up a definite program for the child to acquire some skills. These should be primarily body skills. This program can be used as a means of shifting his environment slightly away from most of the restimulation he is getting. If possible, let the child pick his own program. Help him in setting it up, but if it is specifically designed to be *his* program do not in any way influence its course or insist on its being carried out if he should wish to abandon it. He generally has his reasons, even though he may be unable or reluctant to expose them.

The child needs very little education in Dianetics. The operations are natural for him. He will quickly come to look on his processing as an interesting game if the auditor builds the situation up in this way.

In one respect the auditor can perform a very important function in the education of the child. A child is almost always confused about the world around him largely because of the labels which have been placed on objects by adults who do not understand the serious nature of incorrectly labeling an object for a child. Consider the case of a child who has had no previous data concerning death, and to whom is read the poem about little tin soldiers and angels with golden hair.[4] If this is his first falsely symbolic understanding of the word *death*, then it must be very puzzling to him indeed when he observes how adults really react when death occurs. The impression made by this first misconception about the meaning of death must somehow be obliterated before any accurate communication on the subject can be made to the child. The divergence between this first conception of death and all future conceptions forms a troubled area in the filing system of the analyzer that will tie up some of the child's available attention until the tension is resolved. The technique for accomplishing this is simply to treat the original, incorrect labeling as a lock incident and to lift the tension from it by close present time contact.

Sometimes a lack of semantic orientation will cause problems in the child's mind which have such far-reaching implications that resolving them semantically will produce seemingly miraculous results. One little girl was failing in arithmetic. She was very bright in other subjects, and no reason suggested itself for her failure to do her work in this one subject. She was given a few problems, but became hopelessly bogged down trying to work them out.

Auditor: If an airplane is traveling at 10,000 feet at 2:00 P.M. and at 5,000 feet at 3:00 P.M., how far would a man have to fall to reach the ground at 3:00 P.M.?

---

4. **little tin soldiers and angels with golden hair:** a reference to the poem *Little Boy Blue* by Eugene Field (1850–95), American poet and journalist, known for his children's verse.

Little Girl: *Gee! I dunno. Well, if it's ten thousand and then it's five thousand . . . Honest. I can't tell you. It's really a problem.*

Auditor: Is it just that the problem bothers you?

Little Girl: *I guess so.*

Auditor: Does anyone around here ever talk about problems?

Little Girl: *Well, maybe Mommy might talk about having lots of problems.*

Auditor: Has anyone ever called *you* a problem?

Little Girl: *Well, maybe Mommy might talk about having lots of problems.*

Auditor: Who might call you a problem?

Little Girl: *Well, maybe Mommy. Oh! You mean* that *kind of a problem!*

The word had assumed its right meaning, and the little girl soon started getting good marks in arithmetic.

An auditor may discover information which will make environmental changes necessary for the sake of the child's health. Usually it is possible to obtain the cooperation of the parents in making these changes. If it can be demonstrated to the parent that his child's health will be adversely affected if, for example, he visits his aunt and uncle every summer, the parent will usually discontinue the visit.

Most of the changes necessary in a child's environment will be along the line of removing him from the restimulative effect of allies. The insidious ways in which allies can completely undermine the health and sanity of children without even being aware of what they are doing is hard to imagine unless you have examined the results for yourself.

In one instance an auditor visited a girl in a hospital. When he arrived he found that the grandmother had been there previously, and that the girl had developed a fever. A little questioning established the fact that grandmother and the fever had materialized simultaneously. Straight line memory contacted an illness at nine years of age during which Grandmother had reestablished herself as an ally and insisted that she would be around any time the little girl was sick. When this lock was blown, the fever went down immediately and vanished completely in a few hours.

In this respect it is interesting to note that *any person who countermands the authority of a parent also undermines the independence of the child.* The child's reality consists largely of his relationship to his parents. Any factor which comes between him and his parents is not good for the growth of the child. Any relative or other person who interrupts the communication between a child and his parents, no matter how well-meaning his efforts, and especially if he attempts to set himself up as another less stern parent, is harming the health and sanity of the child. An auditor should use every possible means to have such a person removed from the child's immediate environment.

Dianetics for children has its special problems, too. The

child is not capable of sustained concentration and should not be forced in this regard. Even in working pleasure moments the auditor should be careful not to attempt to keep the child concentrated on one activity any longer than the child can endure without tiring. When it is at all possible, it is better to work every day with a child, since the working period for children must necessarily be shorter. The length of time a child is able to work at one sitting is usually from fifteen minutes to a half hour. Properly prepared, and entering into the spirit of their processing, some children can bear up under it for much longer periods. If the child is unable to concentrate his attention for longer than the average period, it will do no good at all to attempt to keep him beyond that time. In this respect it might be well to note that although working time may have to be cut shorter, the amount of good that can be accomplished even with brief sessions sometimes seems miraculous to persons who have not tried using Dianetic techniques with children.

One problem which exists with children more than with adults is that sometimes one or both of the parents will be actively against Dianetics. If this has extended to the point of using Dianetic terminology in a disparaging way, the task may be made even more difficult. The answer to this problem is, of course, affinity and communication between the auditor and the child. It is good in a case of this kind to emphasize even more the "playing a game" approach, and to avoid use of Dianetic terminology until affinity is well established.

A special problem with a child is that the child will sometimes be unwilling to enter a lock incident which appears light to an adult. One way of getting around this is to ask the child to imagine a television or a movie screen and to picture an incident similar to the lock on this screen. Quite often the actual lock will appear on the screen. One word of warning about this technique (which may also be used with adults on badly occluded locks): *Never tell the child that any part of any situation is imaginary or a delusion.*

Children, even more than adults, lose their grasp on reality when their data are invalidated. If Junior's picture-screen image of Mama has green hair, do not point out to him that Mama's hair is really red. Simply run the lock through and proceed with processing. Eventually the data will begin to straighten out in Junior's mind and he will volunteer the information that Mama's hair is really not green but red, and that he knew it all along.

Nothing in Dianetics provides more thrill than to see a child regain his grasp on reality. Once communication between an auditor and a child has been definitely established, the results of processing are immediately apparent. Children grasp Dianetics easily, and it is not at all uncommon to see them beginning to use the new memory games on Mama and Papa and on play-mates. Unless there is a very bad prenatal bank which has already been keyed in, children's perceptic recalls are usually in good shape. It is a pleasure to watch them regain their own data and reestablish their validity.

Children become particularly adept at running out minor pain incidents immediately after they occur. Since the latest bump or fall may be contacted and the pain lessened or relieved completely by the child himself, several auditors have taught their children the technique of taking such care of minor bruises.

Considering the high adaptability of children, it was not at all surprising when one professional auditor found his little girl out in the backyard, with a look of grim determination on her face, running out the mild spanking her father had just administered!

The problem of processing children is of utmost importance

and will occupy a much greater portion of the auditor's attention than working with adults. Accessibility,[5] parental interference and a child's lack of the right kind of education, all combine to present a real challenge to the auditor—one which only his exercise of deep insight and sphinx-like patience will enable him to meet. He must be firm and at the same time diplomatic with the child's parents. He must meet the child on a companionship level and literally become the child's private tutor. And he must be able to fathom the root of a problem not only from a jumble of information, but from a complete lack of data as well.

It is very interesting that the treatment of a child and the treatment of a psychotic are parallel problems, primarily because both of them present the problem of accessibility. A child that has been rather badly used in his lifetime is prone to resist attention from an adult. He is a problem in self-control because he has not yet learned precision control of his body.

The problem facing the auditor is to direct the child's attention into his own locks and engrams. As the false self-control units or circuits go out, the "I" is more and more able to control the organism. But before a child can be processed his attention must be gathered and focused. When a concentration of the mind on the handling of the body is built up to a sufficient point, the mind can handle the engrams. To accomplish this, a certain amount of reeducation must be undertaken.

Start by getting the child to define words, objects and their uses, and you will find that he has the most confoundedly weird

5. **accessibility:** the state of being willing to be processed (technical sense). The state of being willing to have interpersonal relations (social sense). For the individual himself, accessibility with self means whether or not an individual can recontact his past experiences or data. A man with a "bad memory" (interposed blocks between control center and facsimiles) has memories which are not accessible to him.

misconceptions of the world in which he lives, handed to him by the adults around him. You can straighten out a lot with a child on an educational level alone.

The child's prenatal engram bank is full of engrams that a thirty-five-year-old preclear, with all of his understanding, would hesitate to face. The time track is stoned with parental quarrels, and sometimes sheer brutalities. It is too much to ask that a child of four, five or six years of age face this sort of thing. He cannot do it. His analytical mind is not sufficiently developed, nor does he have a full bank of data with which to evaluate.

Suppose you began processing by taking the child back to a sleigh ride or the time he went swimming. He cooperates, going readily up and down the time track—until you say, "Let's go back to the time when Mama caught you stealing cookies and punished you." Ha! That's one place this kid will not go. It was only a mild licking, very mild—merely had to do with a few slaps when the culprit was anaten from fright. If the child can't go back and face something as mild as this, how can he be expected to go back and face a real knock-down and drag-out fight staged by his parents?

Standard processing, then, is barred to a child until he has been educated into the handling of his own body and has enough data so that he can evaluate. This opens an entirely new line of processing: the identification of objects on an educational level. Simply give the child more data.

Suppose a normal child who catches cold after cold, has asthma,[6] gets very ill, and whose parents say, "We've done

---

6. **asthma:** a chronic disease that makes breathing difficult and causes coughing. Asthma is an allergy characterized by intermittent or continuous difficulty in breathing and a sense of constriction in the chest.

everything in the world for this child," is finally brought in for processing. The best thing to do is to take the child by himself, away from the parents. Ask him to sit down, and talk to him on a rather dignified level. You will find him talking to you on the same dignified level. At that moment you have entered the case.

The most you can do for the child is to build up his confidence and affinity to a point where he will go back and pick up grief. Somebody took his tricycle—a big moment of grief. Once grief is off the case, the chances are that the chronic somatics will disappear, easing up enough tension so the child will become pretty well balanced. Then proof the child against future key-in by telling the parent about restimulation, and the results of emotional upsets which occur in his hearing. Aim for deintensification, not clearing. Your goal is to bring the child up so that he can get along better with his environment.

You will find cases where children are ordered and threatened not to cry, thus sealing in grief. You'll have a difficult time with these children, but you can get back even to this grief area with straight line memory and knock it out.

Once grief has been run and the child has become a little more proficient in playing his memory games, take him back to the last time he was slightly hurt and run it out. Teach him to pick up late-life locks, minor engrams, etc. But don't suppose, because you have gone this far successfully, that you can immediately get back to basic-basic.[7]

If the child is sickly, see if the parents are *really* concerned. Select the most restimulative factors in his environment and get the parents' cooperation in eliminating them. Considerable tact

---

7. **basic-basic:** the first moment of pain, anaten or discomfort in the current life of the individual.

and diplomacy will be required when dealing with parents. One little boy who was very allergic to his mother was being taken to all kinds of health resorts because he was so sickly. Every place he went he carried along the source of his illness. But you couldn't tell Mother in so many words that she was restimulative to her own child, and that he would go right on being sick as long as they were together. Diplomatically try to educate the mother or give her some processing. If the father is the one who is especially interested in the case, sell him on the idea of letting you process the mother first.

You are going to audit a child, but you may wind up by processing one or more adults in the child's vicinity. People will often be so interested in the health of a child that they will permit themselves to be processed for the child's sake when ordinarily they would not bother with processing for their own benefit. And think how much better it would have been for the child if the parents could have been processed *before* their off-spring was conceived.

Don't lecture a child about self-discipline, because this is something that is a native and natural mechanism, not something that is installed with a club. When he begins to get restless and his attention wanders, follow the wandering and let him wander right on out. Don't make processing onerous[8] by demanding that it go longer than the natural span of the child's attention. If you're getting in only as little as five minutes a day, be content. Let him go home if he wants to. Next time you see him he'll be perfectly willing to work with you. If you try to tell him he *has* to have processing, that he *has* to listen to this or that, or *has* to be an obedient boy—you are only contributing to an already handicapped young life.

---

8. **onerous:** burdensome, oppressive or troublesome; causing hardship.

While you are talking to Billy, don't pay any attention to Billy's parents. Above all, don't talk to a parent over the child's head; in fact, it might be advantageous at times to talk to Billy over the head of the parent. Talk only to the child or you will lose all the affinity that must be built up. If the child can talk to you on a different level than he can to others, he will be a different human being, and a much better one after each session.

In Child Dianetics you can expect to need a lot more patience and a lot more endurance than you would in adult processing. You've got to be persistent and be able to adapt your attitude to that of the child. If you can do these things intelligently, Dianetically, you are going to get results.

6

Dianetics
in Child Care

6

Dianetics in Child Care

Dianetic theory generates simple and definite techniques for the handling of children, not only in emergencies, but in ordinary day-by-day care. They can be learned quickly and easily. Working with children is a joy, because they return so easily and naturally and because the results are so visible.

One should try, of course, to keep engrams from forming in the first place. The pregnant woman generally sees to it that nothing happens which might injure the child, and she is usually accorded better care during pregnancy. But she also has a right to ask that people around her not only protect her physically, but see to it that she is not involved in any emotional storms.

Anyone likely to be in contact with a pregnant woman should also be instructed to remain absolutely silent if she happens to suffer some accident or injury. Silence is the first rule, and nothing at all should be said if it can be avoided. She can be helped or ministered to without comment.

A woman who wants her child to have the best possible chance will find a doctor who will agree to keep quiet while examining her and especially during the delivery, and who will insist upon silence being maintained in the hospital delivery room as far as it is humanly possible. She will also want a natural childbirth, and will find a doctor who will cooperate in seeing to it that she has one. A childbirth wherein the mother's pain is not occluded by anesthesia or narcoanesthesia[1] will not be nearly so engramic to the child. Many auditors have found that the first real grief charge lies immediately after birth, due to separation from the mother. If, with the mother under anesthetic, a child is delivered, hurriedly cleaned and taken off to a ward, the break in affinity is severe. Furthermore, it is completely unnecessary.

A doctor who practices natural childbirth will lay the child on the mother's abdomen even before the cord is cut, and as soon as the cord is cut and tied, the mother will give the caressing and nursing. Undoubtedly this procedure will do much to reduce the effect of the sudden affinity break of birth, and probably will eliminate it completely. It is impossible, from a Dianetics point of view, to urge natural childbirth too strongly.

In postnatal life, of course, whether the child is injured or sick, the rule of absolute silence should be kept. The parents should insist that everyone in the child's environment beware of the ally-forming phrases. Anything which might be construed to mean, "You would die without me," or "Everything will be all right so long as I am here," is dynamite, as any auditor knows. Parents who know Dianetics will as sedulously[2] protect their children from people who say such things as they would from wild animals. They will also protect them from all the believe-me-and-everything-will-be-all-right, and you've-got-to-do-as-I-say phrases.

---

1. **narcoanesthesia:** *narco-* meaning sleep and *anesthesia* meaning without feeling. Together this refers to an anesthesia that puts the patient to sleep.

2. **sedulously:** in a manner diligent in application or attention.

Of course, silence around a sick or injured child does not preclude genuine, intelligent affection and physical caresses. The child needs these more than ever when sick, and no amount of loving will form an ally computation if no words are spoken. But caresses are best if gentle and calm. No violent clutching to the breast or mauling should be allowed. Holding a child's hand quietly and firmly rather than agitatedly will give him the assurance of support that he needs when he is sick.

In cases of minor physical injury, anyone around the child may run an assist.[3] But in young children, often just letting them cry out seems to be enough. When a child is hurt, most people find themselves speaking comforting and consoling words almost before they know it. And what they say is usually what they have said a hundred times before when the child was hurt. This restimulates the whole chain of injuries.

Parents can help a child most by saying nothing. It may take a short while to train themselves not to speak when the child is hurt, but it is not difficult to form the habit of remaining silent. Silence need not inhibit affection. One may hold the child, if he wants to be held, or put an arm around him. Often, if nothing is said, a young child will cry hard for a minute or so, and then suddenly stop, smile, and run back to what he was doing. Allowing him to cry seems to release the tension resulting from the injury and no assist is needed if this occurs. In fact, it is often very difficult to make the child return to the moment of injury if he has run it out himself this way. He will avoid the pain of

---

3. **assist:** a simple, easily done process that can be applied to anyone to help them recover more rapidly from accidents, mild illness or upsets; any process which assists the individual to heal himself or be healed by another agency by removing his reasons for precipitating (bringing on) and prolonging his condition and lessening his predisposition (inclination or tendency) to further injure himself or remain in an intolerable condition.

returning as he would the original pain, and probably the incident is already run out and refiled, and therefore no longer important enough to trouble about.

But if the child does not spontaneously recover after a moment or two of crying, then wait until he has recovered from the short period of anaten that accompanies an injury. It is usually not difficult to tell when a child is dazed and when he is not. If he still cries after the dazed period, it is usually because other previous injuries have been restimulated. In this case, an assist is valuable. On older children (five and up) an assist is usually necessary.

When the child is no longer dazed, ask him, "What happened? How did you get hurt? Tell me about it."

As he begins to tell about it, switch him to the present tense if he doesn't tell the story in the present tense spontaneously. Try it this way:

"Well—I was standing on a big rock and I slipped and fell, and . . . " (crying)

"Does it hurt when you are standing on the rock?"

"No."

"What happens when you are standing on the rock?"

"I slip . . . " (crying)

"Then what happens?"

"I fall on the ground."

"Is there grass on the ground?"

"No—it's all sandy."

"Tell me about it again."

You can take the child through it several times until he gets bored or laughs. There is nothing difficult about it, and the whole process may be so casual and easy that anyone unfamiliar with Dianetics will not realize that anything unusual is being done. After a child has had a few assists run this way, he will, upon being injured, run to the person who can administer this painless help and reassurance, demanding to "tell about it."

The best way to keep a child from being restimulated is for the parents to be good Releases or Clears. Unfortunately this takes time. But in the meantime, parents should watch their own dramatizations, especially noting their favorite phrases, and avoid using these as much as possible in the child's presence or to the child himself.

Straight Memory work on each other, aimed at getting rid of recurrent dramatizations and phrases, should help parents to keep highly restimulative scenes down to a minimum until the underlying engrams have been completely run out. This procedure should be applied to any others who are in the child's environment.

Many people habitually tell a child, "Don't do that or you'll get sick," "My goodness, you're certainly getting a bad cold," "You'll get sick if you keep on with that," "I just know Johnny's going to get polio if he goes to school," and countless other such pessimistic suggestions. They also use thousands of "Don'ts," "Can'ts," and "Control yourself" phrases. Parents may watch themselves for these phrases, and avoid their use as much as possible. With a little imagination and practice, it is not difficult to find ways of keeping children safe without using constant verbal restraints which will lock onto underlying engrams. As much as possible, suggestions made to a child should be positive; should appeal to his analytical mind. A child has one, even at an early age. Graphically illustrating what happens to a glass bottle when it drops will get the idea across better than a thousand screams of "Get away from that!" or "Put that down!"

Smooth, gentle motions and a quiet voice will go far toward averting restimulation when children are being handled. Anyone who wishes to work successfully with children will cultivate these attributes. They are particularly valuable in emergencies.

If a child's attention must be obtained quickly because of a potentially dangerous situation developing too far away to enable the guardian to reach the child in a hurry, calling his name loud enough to be heard will do the trick harmlessly. It is much better than screamed injunctions to "Stop!" "Stay there!" "Don't do that!" and so on. It is not nearly so likely to restimulate him.

The technique that will be used most often in dealing with children is informal Straight Memory work. Although it is Straight Memory, often the child will return spontaneously when it is used. Children return so easily that keeping them on memory alone is difficult. But there is no need to prevent them from returning while working straight line.

Straight line memory may be used in hundreds of situations that arise from day to day: whenever the child is fretful, unhappy and crying over something; when he is feeling slightly sick; when he is obviously restimulated by something; when he has overheard a dramatization, or someone has punished him severely or uncorked a dramatization directed toward him; when he feels rejected—in fact, every time a child is unhappy or nervous for any reason or when you know that he has recently had a highly restimulative experience.

The principle here, as in any straight line work, is to get at the specific phrases and situations causing the restimulations. Of course, this technique can be used only after the child has learned to talk enough to give a coherent account of what he is thinking and feeling.

If the child is feeling upset (not seriously ill), you may begin by asking him when he felt this way before. Usually a child will remember. As you ask further questions about what was happening, what he was doing at the time, who was talking, what was said, how he felt, and the usual questions directed toward uncovering the situation, he will describe the scene graphically. When he does so, simply run him through it again a few times. When you come to the end say, "Tell me about it again. Where were you when Daddy was talking?" "Tell it again." Or, simply, "Let's see now, you were sitting on the couch when Daddy says—what did he say?" Any simple phrase which will return the child to the beginning of the scene may be used.

In running children there is no need to use Dianetic terms or to make the thing complex. Children understand, "Tell it again." They love to hear stories over and over again, themselves, and they love to tell their stories to an interested audience. But don't be overly sympathetic. Show affection and interest, yes. But don't croon or moan, "Poor baby, poor little thing!" or similar phrases. They serve only to form sympathy computations.

The more you can enter a child's reality, the better you will be able to help him run locks. Imitate his voice tones, his "Yeah!", "You did!", "And then what?"—adapt yourself to his graphic mimicry, widened eyes, breathless interest or whatever his mood and tone may be—but not to the extent of parroting, of course. If you cannot do it well, then just be simple, natural and interested.

Often, when he is restimulated, a child will use one or two phrases over and over again. To anyone who knows Dianetics he is obviously right in the middle of an engram. In that case you can start with, "Who says that?" or "Who's saying that to you?" or "When did you hear that?"

Sometimes he will insist, "I say it—shut up, you old fool!" or whatever the phrase is. Then ask, "Who else says it?" or "See if you can remember when you heard somebody else say it," and he will usually start telling you about an incident. Patient questioning will usually bring out the last lock on a chain.

One auditor, working with her daughter, was astounded when the child said, "You said it, Mummy, a long time ago." "Where were you when I said it?" "Oh, I was only a little thing—in your tummy." This probably won't happen often. But as the child gets the idea of Straight Memory work and of returning, it may happen sooner or later. Whatever the incident, engram or lock, just go on with questioning to build up the incident. "What were you doing? Where were you? Where was I? What was Daddy saying? What did it look like? What did you feel like?" and so on. Run the child through the incident a few times until he laughs. This will blow the lock and release him from the restimulation.

If the child is crying, a good way to begin is, "What are you crying about?" After a child has told what he is crying about a few times, each time being helped by questioning about the incident, and when his crying has abated, you may ask, "What else are you crying about?" Sometimes, in this way, you may take a child down through a whole chain of locks and possibly even get the key-in.

If the father knows that the child has overheard a dramatization or has been severely punished or scolded, he may run the lock a few hours after the event by asking about it. "Do you remember when I shouted at Mother last night?" If the child is not used to expressing his anger to his parents, or if he has been severely repressed in the past, it may take some coaxing to get him to tell about it. While doing so, try to assure him by your manner that it is perfectly all right for him to talk about it. If he simply cannot, you might try to get him to play it out. If the child plays with dolls or toy animals you may, in play with him, get him to make the dolls or toys act out the dramatization. "This is the mama doll. And this is the little bcy doll. What does the mama doll say when she is mad?" Very often this will take the child right into the scene, and if you let him really open up and describe the scene without condemnation, listening in a sympathetic, interested way, and encouraging him with a well-placed, "Yes . . . and then what?" he will soon drop the pretense and begin to tell you directly what he overheard. Even if he does not do this and, as children often do, he runs over the scene a couple of times with his dolls or toys, it will deintensify to a large extent.

Instead of dolls or toys, you may have the child draw pictures. "Draw me a picture of a woman and a man. . . . What are they doing? Draw me a picture of a woman crying," and so on. The emphasis should always be on the adult who was dramatizing, and not on the child who was naughty. Drawing pictures, playing house with a child: "And then you say . . . And then I say . . . ?" or simply getting the child to make up a story about it will help to get into the lock.

With children who have not been inhibited in their expressions of anger against parents, these subterfuges are not usually necessary. They will tell freely and dramatize scenes they overheard or scoldings they got, if you act as an interested audience and encourage them to build up the scene. If you watch children playing, you will often see them doing exactly that, mimicking their parents and other adults in their dramatizations, and blowing locks for themselves while they do so. Watching children can be an education in Dianetics. Nothing demonstrates Dianetic technique more quickly and forcefully than a child's play. Very often children seem to know how to blow locks for themselves with Straight Memory or by returning over the scene, and will do this by themselves. For severe locks, however, they do need the help of an adult they trust.

Sometimes just asking a child, "What happened to make you feel bad?" or "What did I say to make you feel that way?" will bring out the restimulative elements in the present situation and will take the charge off it and bring him out of the lock.

Occasionally, in exceptional cases, a child may actually recall an engram *on Straight Memory*. If such a return occurs get as much of the engram as possible *on Straight Memory* by using the past tense. Then run pleasure until his tone is high. But do not encourage such a return to an engram until he is prepared for it. It may frighten him and thus inhibit returning later on.

Usually there is no need for caution in this respect. Children will usually bounce right up to present time the minute they come close to a somatic.

If you do not have time to use straight line memory techniques, or if for some other reason you do not wish to, you may bring a child out of a lock by other means. It is easy to recognize when a child is restimulated, and easy to locate him on the Tone Scale. If he is down to a tone of expressed hostility, often you can let him get himself out of it by encouraging him to play out the dramatization.

Everyone is familiar with the violent threats children can

think up when they are frustrated: "I'll tear him to pieces and throw him in the river; I'll make them all go in a closet and lock it up and throw away the key and then they'll be sorry," and so on. If you encourage them by "Yes? And then what will you do?" or "Gee, that would be something!" they will keep on for a while and then they often will suddenly pop right out of the lock and go on with what they were doing.

Or if a child is in an anger tone let him be angry, even if you are the victim. Let him act out his anger, and usually it will disappear quickly. But if you try to suppress it, it will grow worse and last longer, and the whole incident will remain as a lock. Letting a child react to a frustrating situation without further suppression seems to release the energy of the frustration without forming a lock, and will bring him out of it more quickly than almost anything else. Be particularly careful of the "control yourself" phrases at times like these.

If he is in a fear tone, let him tell you about it, giving him all the encouragement you can. This is particularly effective in nightmares. Wake the child, hold him quietly until his crying calms a little, and ask him about the nightmare, taking him through it several times until he is no longer frightened. Then ask him about a pleasure incident, and run that before leaving him. If he doesn't want to sleep alone after that, do not make him face his fear. Stay with him and encourage him to talk about it until he is no longer afraid, even if this takes some time. For chronic fear use Straight Memory techniques again and again, for a few minutes at a time, until you have located and deintensified the underlying locks. In asking about fears, you can locate a series of restimulators by using the phrase "the same as." If the child is afraid of the dark, ask him, "What is the same as dark?" If he is afraid of animals a question will cause him to analyze his fear, and thus you will get at the rest of the content of the engram or lock. Perhaps you will not always be successful on the first questioning, but if you continue patiently you'll soon get an incident that you can help the child run through.

If the child is in a grief tone, "What are you crying about?" will help him to tell you or to act out his grief completely, and to get him out of the lock. Actually, just letting him cry until he gets out of it will often be enough. This is especially true if you are in close contact with him and he knows he can count on you for support and assistance. Don't try to stop a child from crying by simply telling him not to cry. Anyone who has done any auditing knows what damage that does. Either run the incident that caused the crying by asking what happened and getting him to tell about it until he is laughing, or let him cry it out while you caress or hold him. No words in this case; just affection.

If the child is simply fretful and "unmanageable," you can often get him out of the lock by diverting his attention, by introducing a new and fascinating story or picture book or a toy or, in the case of a very young child, something which glitters. This is an old technique, but it is dianetically valid. If the child is fretful, the chances are that he is in the tone of boredom, which means that the particular activity he was interested in has been suppressed somehow. He is looking for something new but is unable to find it. If you can give him something to interest him, his tone will rise quickly. Do not, however, make frantic efforts to attract his attention, plaguing him with jerky movements and such attention diverters as, "See, baby, see the pretty watch!" and if that fails of instantaneous effect, jumping to some other object. This will often only confuse him and act as a further suppressor.[4] Move smoothly and quietly, keep your voice soft and calm, and direct his attention to one new thing. That should be enough.

---

4. **suppressor:** the exterior forces which reduce the chances of the survival of any form.

If none of these work, or if he seems to be solidly set in an engram and dramatizing constantly, you can sometimes free him by bringing him up to present time with intense physical stimulation, like playful wrestling or some other vigorous exercise.

If you can get his attention long enough you can run a pleasure incident by asking him to tell you about some nice thing that happened. He may do it reluctantly at first, but as you encourage it he will often return right into the pleasure incident, and pretty soon his tone will be high again.

Any child can be slowly and smoothly introduced to informal processing by making a new game of remembering. This provides, incidentally, a constructive and pleasant way to keep a child occupied during such odd moments as travelling on street cars, during long trips, waiting, periods of convalescence, and so on.

After all, the immediate aim in clearing a person is to make his past life accessible in every detail. In clearing an adult, hours must sometimes be spent in tuning up perceptics. But children naturally have good perceptic recalls and an immediate ability to return. They love to talk about pleasure moments. A good deal of a child's conversation is filled with the wonderful things he has done or hopes to do, and he often talks spontaneously about incidents where he has been frightened or unhappy.

Making a game an accepted, normal, casual thing of remembering and returning, will help immeasurably when the time comes to do Straightwire work in blowing locks or running assists. When the child has reached the age where he can be formally audited, returning will be a natural and accustomed act, and his case should proceed very swiftly because of this advantage.

Teach a child to run pleasure moments by asking him what

happened when he went to the zoo or went swimming. When he begins to tell you, switch him subtly to present tense, as suggested, if he fails do so himself. Tell him to feel the water, feel himself moving, see what is going on, hear what people are saying and the sounds around him. Build up the perceptics as you would do with an adult. But don't insist on a full perceptic account if the child is running swiftly and surely through the incident, telling about it fluently, and has quite obviously returned as realistically as he can. It doesn't take much to get a child to return, and a few questions directed toward building up somatics and sonic will usually be enough. But don't overlook inserting those few questions each time so that the child gets into the habit of picking up everything.

You can introduce the game by saying, "Let's play remembering," or "Tell me about when you went to," or "Let's pretend we're going to the zoo again," or any other such casual phrase. Enter into the tale as much as you can, adopting the child's tone and manner if you can do it easily, and always being interested and eagerly awaiting the next detail.

When you have practiced on pleasure moments for a few weeks, you can begin blowing locks on a Straight Memory basis, hitting for locks you know are there. "Remember when you were sick last Thanksgiving? Tell me what happened. Who was there? What did so-and-so say?" Or, "Let's see if you can remember when you were frightened by the big dog at school," and so on. When working locks alone, don't let the child return. Stick to past tense. Each time you work a lock in this way, run a pleasure incident or two afterward.

As you continue, you can start going down a chain of locks, trying for the key-in. "Can you remember the first time you were frightened?" "What happened the first time Mother scolded you?"

After a month or so of practice, a child will usually be able to return to early incidents and you will start getting vivid memories of babyhood. Occasionally you may get a mild engram. Run it just as easily and casually as you have the locks, and don't ask the child to close his eyes.

Of course, while you are running locks, you will let the child discharge any grief or fear or anger he experiences without stopping him, and will continue to run the lock until he reaches a tone of boredom or of laughter. All the precautions which apply to the formal auditing of adults are necessary with children: keeping the Auditor's Code, adopting the tone of the incident, and so on.

If the child tends to revivify too vividly, it is a good idea to remind him, "You're just remembering this, you know. It happened a long time ago." With a child who returns too well, it is better to stick to the past tense until he is old enough to understand the whole process. This does not apply to pleasure incidents, which must always be run in present tense.

Whenever a child comes to tell you about an accident he had or something that frightened him or made him unhappy, listen to it and run over it several times. As children learn how to "play remembering" and learn what it does for them, they will begin to ask for runs when they want or need them.

If a child, from the time he has been able to talk, has been taught to remember and to return to pleasure incidents, it can be predicted that he will be ready for formal auditing at an early age. The criteria for starting formal auditing are that the child understand the significance of prenatal life, know about birth, and realize that repeated running of a painful experience will dispose of it forever. When the child is willing to face a mild pain in order to avoid later pain, formal auditing can begin. In the case of seriously disturbed children, formal auditing may of sheer necessity be started before the child understands these things. In such cases there must be established a high degree of affinity between auditor and child in order to contact and reduce engrams successfully.

Summary

The main points in Dianetic child care are:

1. Prevention of engrams in the unborn child through proper care of the expectant mother, silence during any injury or illness she may suffer, and avoidance of ally-forming phrases.

2. Running assists on minor injuries to the young child, if necessary or letting the child cry it out if that seems to be enough.

3. Blowing locks via straight line memory, by getting the child to remember the last time it happened, or by getting him to tell you in full what happened that made him unhappy.

4. Teaching a child to remember and return by running pleasure moments.

5. Using pleasure moments or other techniques for bringing the child out of locks up to present time.

Such care will prepare the child for formal auditing, will make formal auditing easy and rapid when it can be begun, will clear out most of the lock material before formal running, and will keep the child healthier and happier.

7

An Auditor's Report

7

An Auditor's Report

The preclear is a young boy, age seven. He was referred to the auditor for the specific purpose of trying to discharge a chronic somatic, asthma. The boy has had a total of approximately three hours of processing over a period of five weeks.

The following are data as gathered from the preclear:

"When I get pretty tired at night I wake up and I'm wheezing. I get cross and start hitting my brother. My mother says, 'Now, now, cut it out.'"

When asked how he feels, in present time, he usually answers, "Okay. Not bad. Pretty good."

The preclear was returned to the first time he ever heard the word *asthma*. He found himself on the doctor's couch and heard his mother say to the doctor, "What do you think is the matter, doctor?" The doctor's answer was, "He has asthma. He must be kept quiet." This was run over several times in reverie and a few times in straight line memory work.

The preclear was then directed to an earlier incident in which his mother might have told his doctor, or in which a doctor might have told his mother anything about asthma or any other illness. At the age of one he picked up his mother saying, "You're a sick little boy. Stay here and be quiet and you'll get better."

Asked how he felt on the doctor's table he said, "Not so very good."

At this point the preclear was guided into present tense. Mother says to the preclear, "I'll fix that."

Preclear says to Mother, "I don't want to drink that medicine."

Mother says, "Ha, ha, it's not medicine. It's jelly juice. It will make you feel better."

The preclear contacts the feeling of drinking and says, "That's good."

This episode in the doctor's office was contacted several times in three different sessions.

From observation of the preclear the auditor believes that the boy's general tone seems slightly improved—a tone of 3 plus most of the time. His mother reports that he gets along better with her, with his father and with other members of the family. He has not had an attack of asthma for the last two months, although the auditor was told that his attacks came quite frequently before processing was begun. On the nights that he awakens with somewhat of a "wheeze" in his breathing, it is less intense than formerly, and it is gone by morning.

Several locks have been sprung on the preclear, particularly control phrases or locks which contain control phrases such as

"Now take it easy and you will feel better," which was laid in by the mother; "Now take it easy," laid in by the father when the child was five months old; and "Now control your knobs," laid in by the mother—"knobs" meaning ears. The child does have large ears, and is not a handsome child. At his birth the mother made the statement, "It's a boy. My, but he's ugly!"

Other locks with control phrases that have been blown are "Lower your volume," meaning "Control the tone of your voice," and "Be a good boy," which was contacted at one month postnatal. "Lower your volume" was contacted two months postnatally. "Now control your knobs" was located at eleven months postnatal. To date, this auditor has not gone into the prenatal engram bank.

Asked what asthma is, the preclear answers, "It is a sickness. I don't like it. I don't want to have it." Asked if he needs to have asthma, he says, "No." To the question, "Do you need to wheeze?" he answered, "I think about how good it will feel when I stop."

The child's mother has been able to pick up in straight line memory the fact that she suffered from acute bronchitis during the fourth month of the preclear's prenatal existence. She received treatment from an osteopath[1] friend. During these treatments there was much talking, usually local gossip. She remembers saying, "I cough so hard, I'm so afraid I'll have a miscarriage. I don't see how it can stay put. I feel as though I'll cough it out. I have such a tight feeling in my chest."

---

1. **osteopath:** a person who specializes in osteopathy, the treatment of disease chiefly by manipulation of the bones and muscles. Osteopathy also includes all types of medical and physical therapy. Osteopathy is based on the concept that the structure and functions of a body and its organs are interdependent and any structural deformity may lead to functional breakdown.

During the last session with the preclear, he was asked what happens when he gets an attack. The phrase that came out was "I get such a tight feeling in my chest." When asked to describe this feeling he said, "It feels like there is something on top of me." Asked if he could feel it now, he said, "No, but I can remember how it feels." Asked to describe it again, he began to feel this pressure on his chest. He was urged merely to describe the pain. He said the pain was not very bad and that it went away almost as soon as he told the auditor about it. There was apparently a slight return, and a bouncer which took him up toward present time. Rather than work the child when he was comparatively tired, the bouncer was left in effect and pleasure run to alleviate restimulation. When he left the last session he felt considerably better.

Seven weeks later the auditor had an opportunity to run a short straight line session with the child in which he stated that he felt very well, and that he hadn't had asthma for several weeks. He was not taking any more pills, except for vitamins, and he said, "I like Mommy and Daddy and my brother more than I ever did."

Without consultation with the child's auditor, and without seeing his report, the mother of this preclear reports substantially as follows:

"Since his processing my child has shown a definite rise in spirits. He enjoyed the psychometric[2] testing very much, had excellent affinity with the psychometrist. The length, intensity and duration of his daytime periods of rage or frustration have decreased. His father has also noticed this.

---

2. **psychometric:** of or having to do with *psychometry,* the measurement of the duration, force, interrelations, or other aspects of mental processes, as by psychological tests.

"It seems as though he has developed some understanding of his own and my displays of rage, and will sometimes stand patiently and wait for me to finish! This may be due to processing or to his growing understanding of the discussions and comments he hears constantly at home. The most dramatic change in the past four weeks, however, from my standpoint, is his behavior at night.

"It has been customary for several years for him to be disturbed around two or three o'clock in the morning by the need to urinate and to clear his nose and throat. These periods began with a baby's angry cry, and it took from five to thirty minutes to wake him up enough to go to the bathroom. For four weeks he has not had this difficulty. He calls me by the squalling, but is awake when I get to his room, goes to the bathroom chatting cheerfully, snorts and snuffles a few times, and goes back to bed and to sleep. He has even slept straight through the night, perhaps seven times so far.

"Whether this is attributable to two or three fifteen-minute sessions a week, I don't know. He had resisted auditing for a while and had a mild asthma attack for two days, but no more night trouble.

"Of course, my own attitude is constantly improving; my displays of anger are less frequent and less violent."

8

Special Technique
for Children

8

Special Technique for Children

A child's processing must necessarily take a somewhat different form from that of the Standard Procedure available for older children and adults. The child can no more realize the importance of processing than he can understand the necessity of remaining off the roof of a barn or avoiding a dead limb when climbing the neighbor's cherry tree. His is a world of limited data of comic books and television, of seeking always the most pleasurable experiences and avoiding those which invariably bring him pain. It is a rare child, indeed, who understands the implications of the smallpox vaccination, how by the simple course of bearing up to a pin scratch now he won't have a terrible sickness later. He sees only the pin, and feels only the pain of now; tomorrow is a long way off and he can't see and feel tomorrow.

His span of attention is limited. A brand-new toy jeep will keep him interested for a few hours at most, and then he must seek something else. A simple household task such as raking leaves, even though done with the promise of a shining 25-cent piece, is easily forgotten if something new comes along at just the right moment. The future is yet to come, but this new diversion is here now. Besides, Father sometimes makes him save the quarter—a laudable[1] attribute for a child—but what does he

---

1. **laudable:** deserving praise; praiseworthy; commendable.

get for working so hard, for giving up his play time with other youngsters whose parents are somewhat more lenient? The promise that the quarter will be one cent greater next year is a poor substitute for a whirl around the block in somebody's Irish mail.[2]

Communication between the child and the adults around him has a considerable lack of reality. Time and time again a parent will invalidate a child's statement, one which he knows beyond all doubt is true and browbeat the child into accepting the adult version. "Now, Billy, you know that isn't right! Mother knows best." He has been confronted with the datum that Mother knows just about all there is to know about the world outside, and when something he believes to be true, beyond a shadow of doubt is declared absolutely false by Mother, he is more than confused. And when Father does the same thing, reality in the child's world takes a new low.

His education is limited by his years. He has learned the language or some of it and is only just learning to associate words and phrases with the realities of the world about him. One thing he has learned the hard way—to avoid pain. If, in processing, he repeatedly runs up against a painful incident and feels the somatics of a previously painful experience, it isn't long before he avoids processing itself as a painful experience.

With his limited span of attention, his difficulty of communication in an adult sense, and his lack of education taken into account, Standard Procedure must be adapted to his years. Patience is perhaps the most important ingredient of all when processing a child. It will require many hours to make up for just one loss of temper, of just one outburst of rage because Betty doesn't do things quite the way you think she should.

---

2. **Irish mail:** a toy handcar.

Consider, for example, a child of five. The child, from his own viewpoint, has been badly badgered throughout his short span of years and has been pushed around by the adults. You should provide something which will, in effect be educational first of all. Therefore, set aside a time during the day when the child can do anything he desires which doesn't hurt animals or property. If he wants you around during this time, which you can begin to call "Billy's time," fine. Spend the hour or two with him and do whatever he asks you to do, within reason of course. After the novelty wears off he will begin to use "his" time to ask you questions about the world around him, questions which you should answer very carefully and accurately, no matter what the subject might be. It would be very unfair to say, in answer to an innocent question about sex for instance, "Now let's don't talk about nasty things like that." Answer him simply and fully, and with an absolute minimum of stammering and blushing on your part.

Sometimes the child will want to spend "his" time being held on your lap, and the special case might even want a bottle. Don't tell him this is childish, and that he has outgrown such pursuits. Give him the bottle and hold him on your lap until he tires of this.

Perhaps he will want to dramatize family difficulties, such as a recent argument between his parents. Fine. Go over it with him just as he desires. This will often release many locks formed during the unpleasant experience, not only those formed in the child but, if you are the parent involved, in yourself as well. When the child becomes assured that there are no strings attached to your offer of "his" time, he will take full advantage of the opportunity to go over many details which have hurt him, and once returned to in this fashion, they will seldom bother him again.

Then, after a few periods spent in this way, ask if there is anything he wants to know, or anything he wants to talk about. Allow his dignity and enormous self-determinism to assert itself. Coax him to explain things to you, in his own language. When he runs across something which troubles him for a meaning, he will ask you, if you have gained his confidence. Sometimes when the child asks you a question which you are sure he should have known for some time, feed it back to him as another question, asking him what he thinks about it. This is often what the child really wants, and is only using the question as a means of opening discussion on the subject.

During "his" time, don't ask *why* a certain thing happened, ask *what* happened. *Explain* why. If there is a need for giving him information use multivalued logic (right-maybe-wrong) and explain its use. As for the decisions which are made about any discussion, let him make his own decision, and do not tell him he is wrong. If you feel he has made a decidedly false assumption, save your comments for another period, and feed the appropriate questions, explanations and data again.

Single-valued explanations or definitions are actually positive suggestion. To say a thing is unqualifiedly true is to attempt to make a child accept your decision about a subject. Never forget the qualifying data—"The *dictionary* says that white is the combination of all colors." "*Grandmother* told me she has never seen Pike's Peak." By so saying the child is allowed to make his own evaluation as to whether or not the dictionary is right, or as to whether or not Grandmother ever actually visited Pike's Peak. It might just be that Grandmother told you one thing, and gave someone else another version.

The tone level of a child might be described as his "spirit," or attitude toward life in general. If he is in a high tone, he will be happy, seldom crying, healthy and energetic. If he is in a low tone he will give the appearance of being continually sad about something, rarely giving himself over completely to playing with other children, and if not sickly and ill, certainly very nearly so. The tone level of either adult or child runs from apathy, or total disinterest in anything, through anger and overaggressiveness, to partial good spirits and at the top of the Tone Scale, bubbling enthusiasm. Thus it can be seen that merely because a child is quiet there is no reason to assume he is in better shape than when he is angry about something. He might well be in the apathy range of the Tone Scale—and this is a very dangerous level to be in, from the point of view of the child's general health and well-being.

From a short study of the Tone Scale which follows it will be possible for you to place your child rather accurately as to his attitude toward life:

Overall Pattern of Tone Scale in Descending Order

Tone 4: Eager pursuit of activity, with complete freedom of choice for other activities as desired.

Interested pursuit of activity, some doubt as to complete freedom in other activities, some doubt as to ability to overcome suppressor on activity being pursued.

Hesitant pursuit of activity, greater doubt of ability to overcome suppressor or find other lines of activity.

Tone 3: Continued, dogged pursuit of activity, hope of overcoming suppressor only with effort.

Indifference to activity—mild attempts to find other fields of action.

Withdrawal from activity being suppressed, direction of other lines of activity remaining open.

Tone 2: If other activity closed, the situation suddenly changes. The individual must find a way out of the suppressed activity before he again has any freedom of choice. The decision is made for him, as it were, by the inhibition laid on by the suppressor. At this point he attempts to destroy the suppressor with relatively mild efforts.

If these efforts do not succeed, he makes violent efforts to destroy the suppressor.

If the suppressor is still unconquered, his field of action is constricted even more, for now he cannot even act directly against the suppressor, and he enters the tone level where he tries to find ways of destroying the suppressor by delayed action. Fear begins here, since there is a strong doubt as to whether the suppressor can ever be destroyed.

Tone 1: As fear increases and the possibility of destroying the suppressor becomes more and more remote, the individual makes violent attempts to escape in any way possible.

If he cannot escape, his last recourse is a frantic cry for help. Grief, sobbing, tears seem to be such a cry—especially evident in young children. In case of loss of an ally, grief seems to be a desperate attempt to bring the ally back, a call for help to the ally.

If the call for help fails and his cry is unanswered, there is nothing further the individual can do, and he enters the tone of apathy, submitting finally to the suppressor.

Tone 0: If the suppressor continues, apathy increases, becoming paralysis, unconsciousness and finally, death.

The importance of placing your child's level on the Tone Scale is many-fold. For one thing, it will suggest very quickly a likely area of charge or emotional distress. For another, as processing continues, you have available a means for checking the progress of your work and efforts. If for instance, your child should become generally angry after a few sessions of processing, you need not immediately feel that because of this he is getting worse instead of better. Perhaps he was in apathy level before you began. It will be quite the natural thing for him to rise through anger, and thence to more eager pursuits of activity.

From a study of the Tone Scale a few methods of processing may suggest themselves. Suppose a child is low in tone, perhaps crying. Try diverting his attention to some other field of activity instead of offering cooing words of sympathy. In many cases it is surprising to see the sudden cessation of tears and the interest in the new object of attention. Of course, this will not work if too much attention is tied up in the lock or key-in which is the basis of his crying. As soon as the diverting influence is removed, or he tires of the new activity or interest, his attention is once again pulled down into the causative incident. When this method is used it corresponds very closely to bringing an adult "up to present time."

In the case of a heavy lock into which his diverted attention is drawn time and again, establish communication with him as soon as you can, and then ask what happened. Get him to tell you three or four times exactly what happened, and the tone will rise very quickly. This may be used often, in or out of regular session times.

There are children who, when they have been slightly hurt in play with other youngsters or even with themselves and their toys, will break into tears and cry far in excess of the seriousness of the incident. Offer the child little sympathy at this time, but, rather, ask her what happened. "How did you fall? Oh, I see. Were you running at the time? And where did the pedal scratch you? Now tell me about it again." It will require no more than three or four recountings before the child becomes so bored with the incident that she is anxious to resume her play. A few instances like this and she soon gets the idea. Either she won't bother to run in and cry about a trivial bump, or she will determinedly go over it a few times by herself. A "crybaby" will in this way become a quiet, happy child in a very short while.

In order to keep the child's tone high while processing, a series of memory games may be played. They will demonstrate how pleasant it can be to keep in contact with the past, and will be educational as well. Sometimes a series of cards about the size of the ordinary bridge deck is used, each showing a large capital letter on its face. The cards are shuffled, and the child asked to close his eyes. A number of the cards are then laid out side by side, face up, with the letters in full view. The child is allowed a five- or ten-second look, and then the cards are turned over. In a surprisingly short time the child can name up to a dozen letters in sequence, and will enjoy the success immensely. If the child asks you to play the game, too, don't back down because you are afraid you cannot do as well. Do the best you can. Perhaps in at least one tiny field the child will find something he can actually do better than an adult. It will do wonders for his tone.

There is one subject which has been mentioned from time to time in this book, but which has not been dealt with extensively—the existence of prenatal engrams. Sometimes when children are asked to return to some incident in which a small amount of pain or grief exists, they slip naturally back in memory to prebirth existence. They speak glibly of their life within Mother's "tummy," and describe sounds and other perceptions with as vivid a recollection as talking about yesterday's birthday party.

Prenatal engrams do, definitely, exist. In fact, the earlier ones form the basic painful experience upon which hundreds of later engrams group together in chains, perhaps on the strength of one word common to each, or on the strength of a similar perceptic content. To send a child back to one of these basic engrams, however, would be tantamount to asking him to walk between a couple of fighting lumberjacks. Until he has gained the age of eight to twelve years, and has had considerable experience in running minor engrams, it is definitely advisable to restrict the processing to straight line memory. If he contacts one in memory and leaves it immediately of his own accord, do not send him back to it. If he contacts it naturally and it does not frighten him excessively, the chances are you can run it although caution is advised. Far more analytical data than is contained in the average child's mind is needed to give reality to prenatal engrams.

There are a number of things to guard against if you wish the child to continue his processing. One of these is positive suggestion. The fertile imagination of children makes them vulnerable to a statement which says a thing is true or false, black or white. Try always to maintain an attitude that a thing *may* be true or false, that there are always qualifiers. One example of positive suggestion which is rather pernicious,[3] and which unfortunately is used all too often is "Jimmy's a Catholic. He isn't nice."

You as the child's auditor must always be careful not to display any signs that you are restimulated, or emotionally affected, by any of the material from the child's reactive mind. It is only natural that such be the case, particularly if you are the parent, but a good "poker face" in an event like this is worth its weight in gold. Sometimes a child will blow a lock or, in finer language, destimulate a lock, by making ugly noises with his mouth. It became a lock in the first place because Papa objected.

---

3. **pernicious:** causing insidious harm or ruin; ruinous; injurious; hurtful.

When this occurs, sit through it, giving no sign that you are in the least affected.

Be particularly careful that you always keep your end of a bargain. Never tell a child you will be with him at "his time" tomorrow, and then not show up, or try to put him off. It will cause a break in affinity every time, and such breaks are very difficult to mend. Make no bargain with a child which you are not certain you can keep.

Guard against a sugary attitude during processing, and then a "hands off" attitude at any other time. Dianetic attitude should continue throughout every day. Even though 1:30 in the afternoon is not "his time," speak civilly to him anyway, and answer his questions just as though he were in processing. He will soon make an evaluation that "your time" is somehow just a little bit different than "his time."

And now for points of attack. If there are any strange, out-of- the ordinary activities in which your child engages, search for the reasons behind these actions. The chances are that they are dramatizations of adult actions, perhaps your own. Viewed Dianetically, the actions of a child often surprise a parent, in that they turn out to be the parent's own dramatizations. So discovered, it is then expedient to have them "run out" of the parent as soon as possible. Although it is helpful to the child to run them as locks, unless the parent ceases the dramatization, the chances are good that a new lock will be installed in the very near future.

An informal quiz, either in writing or verbally given, often helps locate areas of emotional stress in a child. Parental punishment usually installs a childhood lock, and a quiz concerning punishments nearly always is fertile ground for a processing session. Ask him the reasons for the punishment, and what he thinks about the justice of the incident. But do not try to justify your idea of justice.

A quiz as to times when his data was invalidated is usually very productive of locks. Go back over, in your own mind, times when you told him he was wrong about something, when he came to you bubbling with enthusiasm and you threw a mantle[4] of despondency over him by telling him he was utterly wrong. Ask in the quiz whether something he had wanted very much to do was denied him by someone. Also any time in which his dignity was profaned[5]—such as a remonstrance[6] for nakedness in the company of others.

All of these things, and many others, will lead you unerringly to moments in the child's past in which locks have been installed.

Sometimes the question arises as to when to begin a Dianetic attitude around a child. Actually, it begins with Preventive Dianetics—before conception. While the child is being carried, the mother should consider the effects of grief, arguments, fights and other engram-forming activities. The father and others in the mother's immediate surroundings should also be cognizant of the effects of an engram, and how one of these is formed. Grandmothers who engage in monologue during Mother's morning sickness should be gently headed for the door. During birth an absolute minimum of noise and conversation should be permitted. And then in the child's early postnatal months care, should be taken to remain silent during bumps, sicknesses or other childhood ills.

In short, the Dianetic attitude should be practiced twenty-four hours a day, seven days a week.

---

4. **mantle:** something that covers, envelops or conceals.

5. **profaned:** treated (sacred things) with irreverence or contempt.

6. **remonstrance:** the act of speaking, reasoning or pleading in complaint or protest.

9

Sessions with Children

9

Sessions with Children

The following is a verbatim account of several Dianetic processing sessions or portions of sessions with children. Its purpose is to show how an auditor may work with children who are old enough for processing in reverie.

Nephew Jimmy, age ten and a half, has been showing the auditor his workbench and the model airplanes he is currently building. Jimmy knows that his uncle is an HDA,[1] but doesn't know what Dianetics is. He has a great deal of affinity for his uncle.

Auditor: Very nice. Say, let's try some Dianetics.

Jimmy: *Okay. What do I do?*

Auditor: Make yourself comfortable on the bed. Take off your shoes. *(Jimmy does this.)* You want a pillow? Are you comfortable?

Jimmy: *I don't need a pillow. I'm all right.*

---

1. **HDA:** an abbreviation for Hubbard Dianetics Auditor, a person who has been trained to deliver auditing as described in *Dianetics: The Modern Science of Mental Health.*

Auditor: You will remember all that happens. All right. You may close your eyes. If the light is too bright, you may put one arm over your eyes. *(Jimmy does this.)* Now, let's return to a very pleasant incident. *(Pause.)* What are you doing?

Jimmy: *I was playing with my dog in the back yard.*

Auditor: What is your dog's name?

Jimmy: *Spike.*

Auditor: What do you hear?

Jimmy: *My dog was barking.*

Auditor: What else do you hear?

Jimmy: *Cars going by in the street.*

Auditor: Is anyone talking?

Jimmy: *No.*

Auditor: Is anyone else there?

Jimmy: *Yes, my mother was hanging up the wash.* (Jimmy remains aware of the reality of the incident as something that happened to him in the past. Continues to use past tense and yet returns efficiently. Perceptics seem to be good.)

Auditor: What are you doing?

Jimmy: *Playing with my dog.*

Auditor: Is it fun?

Jimmy: *Yes.*

Auditor: What sort of a day is it?

Jimmy: *Warm.*

Auditor: What happens next?

Jimmy: *I go in the house.*

Auditor: Let's return to the beginning of the incident and go through it again.

Jimmy: *I was in the back yard. I was playing with my dog. After a while I go in the house.*

Auditor: Return to the beginning and go through it again.

Jimmy: *I was in the yard.*

Auditor: What do you hear?

Jimmy: *The cars going by and my dog barking.*

Auditor: Are you saying anything?

Jimmy: *No.*

Auditor: How old are you?

Jimmy: *Three.*

Auditor: Continue.

Jimmy: *I pet my dog and then I go in the house.*

Auditor: How do you feel?

Jimmy: *Fine.*

Auditor: Let's go now to a pleasant incident when you were a little older. *(Pause.)* What are you doing?

Jimmy: *I was out on the front lawn. My picture was being taken.*

Auditor: Who's taking the picture?

Jimmy: *My father.*

Auditor: What's he wearing?

Jimmy: *Blue pants and a white shirt.*

Auditor: Is anyone else there?

Jimmy: *Yes. My mother and sister. They are in the picture.*

Auditor: What is being said?

Jimmy: *Father says, "Smile."*

Auditor: Can you hear the camera click?

Jimmy: *Yes.*

Auditor: What else?

Jimmy: *Cars going by.*

Auditor: What happens now?

Jimmy: *We went to Sunday School.*

Auditor: Who goes with you?

Jimmy: *My mother and sister.*

Auditor: How about your father?

Jimmy: *He doesn't go.*

Auditor: Go back to the beginning and run through it again.

Jimmy: *I was out on the front lawn.*

Auditor: How old are you here?

Jimmy: *Five.* (The auditor has Jimmy roll through the incident several times. Jimmy's sister Mary and another girl, Judy, both aged twelve, enter while the incident at age five is being rerun, making some noise.)

Auditor: Do you know what happened just now, Jimmy?

Jimmy: *My sister and Judy came in.*

Auditor: Did it disturb you?

Jimmy: *No.*

Auditor: Is it all right to demonstrate for them?

Jimmy: *Sure.* (The auditor has Jimmy rerun the incident at five, including the disturbance caused by entrance of sister and girlfriend.)

Auditor: All right, let's return to a pleasant incident, which happened when you were a little baby. What are you doing?

Jimmy: *I was in the crib.*

Auditor: Anyone else there?

Jimmy: *No. I was supposed to sleep, but I didn't.*

Auditor: What are you thinking?

Jimmy: *Oh . . . about what to do.*

Auditor: Is it pleasant?

Jimmy: *Yes.*

Auditor: How is the room?

Jimmy: *Warm. The shades are pulled down.*

Auditor: What are you wearing?

Jimmy: *Diapers.*

Auditor: Let's return to the beginning of the incident when your mother puts you to bed. What are you doing?

Jimmy: *I was in the front room on the floor.*

Auditor: What happens?

Jimmy: *Mother came in the room and picked me up.*

Auditor: Can you feel her lift you?

Jimmy: *Yes.*

Auditor: Does she say anything?

Jimmy: *"It's time for you to go to bed."*

Auditor: How old are you?

Jimmy: *Six months.*

Auditor: Let's come up to present time. How old are you?

Jimmy: *Ten.*

Auditor: What's your age?

Jimmy: *Ten.*

Auditor: Give me a number.

Jimmy: *Ten.*

Auditor: All right. You may open your eyes. *(Jimmy sits up.)* How did you like it?

Jimmy: *Fine! Say, Unc, what is this Dianetics?*

Auditor: Why, it's a process whereby you return to incidents in your past life and visit them over again. Was it fun?

Jimmy: *Yes.*

Auditor: Mary, would you like to try?

Mary: *No.*

Auditor: Why not? It's fun.

Jimmy: *Yeah, why don't you?*

Mary: *Well . . . I don't know. Oh, all right.*

Auditor: Make yourself comfortable on the bed. *(Mary does.)* Close your eyes. You may put your arm over your eyes if the light is too bright. You will remember what happens. Let's return to an incident that happened when you were much smaller. *(Pause.)* What are you doing?

Mary: *Nothing.*

Auditor: What do you see?

Mary: *Nothing.*

Auditor: All right, let's return to a pleasant incident at about the age of three, as Jimmy did. *(Pause.)* What are you doing?

Mary: *Nothing. I can't do anything.*

Auditor: Yes, you can. Try it and see. *(Pause.)* Now, what are you doing?

Mary: *I was out at the side of the house. My picture is being taken.*

Auditor: Who's taking your picture?

Mary: *Mother.*

Auditor: Is anyone else there?

Mary: *No.*

Auditor: What does your mother say?

Mary: *"Smile."*

Auditor: Can you hear the camera click?

Mary: *Yes.*

Auditor: What happens then?

Mary: *A station wagon drives up and we get in it to go to Sunday School.*

Auditor: What is your mother wearing?

Mary: *A green and white dress.* (The auditor has Mary run through the incident several times, then asks Mary to go to a pleasure moment at about the age of one.)

Mary: *I was on the floor in the dining room, resting in a playpen.*

Auditor: What are you doing?

Mary: *I'm gurgling.*

Auditor: Can you hear anything else?

Mary: *There's someone talking in the front room.*

Auditor: Who is it?

Mary: *I don't know.*

Auditor: Is your mother there?

Mary: *I don't know.*

Auditor: Yes or no—is your mother there?

Mary: *Yes.*

Auditor: Who else?

Mary: *I don't know.*

Auditor: Is it another woman?

Mary: *Yes.*

Auditor: What are they talking about?

Mary: *I don't know.*

Auditor: What do you hear them saying?

Mary: *I hear them talking, but I don't know what they're saying.*

Auditor: Listen closely. What are they saying?

Mary: *It sounds like French.*

Auditor: Does your mother talk French?

Mary: *No, but it sounds like French.*

Auditor: All right. Let's return to the beginning of the incident and go through it again. *(The auditor has Mary go through the incident several times and then brings her up to present time.)*

Auditor: Come up to present time . . . How old are you?

Mary: *Twelve.*

Auditor: What is your age?

Mary: *Twelve.*

Auditor: Give me a number.

Mary: *Twelve.*

Auditor: You may open your eyes. How do you feel?

Mary: *All right.* (Chuckles.)

Auditor: Now, what about you, Judy; would you like to try? *(Both of the other children urge her to try and she agrees. The auditor returns her to an incident at about the age of three.)*

Auditor: What are you doing?

Judy: *I am playing with my dolls.*

Auditor: Where are you?

Judy:	*I am on the blanket.*
Auditor:	Where are you?
Judy:	*In this little park.*
Auditor:	Is anyone there with you?
Judy:	*Yes. My mother.*
Auditor:	What is your mother doing?
Judy:	*She's sleeping.*
Auditor:	And what are you doing?
Judy:	*Playing with my dolls.*
Auditor:	What do you hear?
Judy:	*Cars are going by. People are walking.*
Auditor:	What do you say to your dolls?
Judy:	*Nothing.*
Auditor:	Let's go back to the beginning of this incident and go through it again. *(Judy does this several times.)*
Auditor:	How do you feel?
Judy:	*Fine.*
Auditor:	Let's go now to an incident at about the age of seven. What are you doing?

Judy: *I'm swimming in this pool with my girlfriend.*

Auditor: Where is this?

Judy: *In the mountains. We are having a vacation and I am swimming with my girlfriend.*

Auditor: What's her name?

Judy: *Barbara.*

Auditor: How's the water?

Judy: *It's cold.*

Auditor: Are you enjoying yourself?

Judy: *Yes, it's fun.*

Auditor: How old are you?

Judy: *Seven.*

Auditor: All right, let's come up to present time. How old are you?

Judy: *Nine.*

Auditor: Let's come up to present time. What is your age?

Judy: *Twelve.*

Auditor: Give me a number.

Judy: *Ten.*

Auditor: Come all the way up to present time. Now what's your age?

Judy: *Twelve.*

Auditor: How old are you?

Judy: *Twelve.*

Auditor: Let me have a number.

Judy: *Twelve.*

Auditor: Open your eyes. How do you feel?

Judy: *All right.* (The children agree that returning was fun, and go in to supper. After supper, the auditor talks alone to Jimmy about Dianetics. Jimmy habitually wets the bed.)

Auditor: Do you still wet the bed?

Jimmy: *Yes.*

Auditor: How old were you when it first started?

Jimmy: *Oh, I guess I was about seven.*

Auditor: Remember the first time you did it?

Jimmy: *Yes.*

Auditor: Anyone else in your family wet the bed?

Jimmy: *No.*

Auditor: All right, let's find out more about it. Make yourself comfortable. Take off your shoes.

Jimmy: *Okay.*

Auditor: Let's return to the first time you wet the bed. What are you doing?

Jimmy: *Ah . . .* (Pause.)

Auditor: Are you asleep?

Jimmy: *Yes.*

Auditor: What happens?

Jimmy: *I was asleep. I was dreaming. Then I woke up. The bed was wet. I got up and went to the bathroom. Then I came back and put a blanket on the bed.*

Auditor: Return to the beginning. You are dreaming?

Jimmy: *Yes.*

Auditor: What are you dreaming about?

Jimmy: *A BB gun.*

Auditor: Yes or no—is this the first time you wet the bed?

Jimmy: *No.*

Auditor: Let's return to the first time you wet the bed. What happens?

Jimmy: *I was asleep. I was dreaming.*

Auditor: What are you dreaming about?

Jimmy: *A BB gun. I dreamed about BB guns all that year.* (This auditor immediately sees a likeness between "BB" and "baby."

Auditor: How old are you?

Jimmy: *Seven.*

Auditor: How much earlier is this than the other time?

Jimmy: *The week before.*

Auditor: Who in your family told you you were a big baby?

Jimmy: *My father.*

Auditor: Let's return to the first time your father told you this. What are you doing?

Jimmy: *I was fighting with Mary.*

Auditor: What happens?

Jimmy: *She slapped me and I started to cry.*

Auditor: What does your father say?

Jimmy: *"You're a big baby."* (The child was a big baby at birth, over ten pounds.)

Auditor: What else?

Jimmy: *"Go take a bath and go to bed."*

Auditor: How old are you now, while this is happening?

Jimmy: *Six.*

Auditor: Answer yes or no—is this the first time your father says this to you?

Jimmy: *Yes.*

Auditor: What happens later that night after you go to bed?

Jimmy: *I'm dreaming and I wake up. The bed is wet.*

Auditor: Yes or no—is this the first time you wet the bed?

Jimmy: *Yes.*

Auditor: Return to the scene with your sister. What do you hear?

Jimmy: *My sister and I were fighting.*

Auditor: Does she say anything to you?

Jimmy: *"You're a big dope."*

Auditor: What do you say?

Jimmy: *I call her a big dope. Then she hits me in the face.*

Auditor: Can you feel it?

Jimmy: *Yes.*

Auditor: What do you do?

Jimmy: *I start to cry.*

Auditor: What does your father say?

Jimmy: *"You're a big baby. Go take a bath and go to bed."*

The auditor runs this lock as an engram several times, runs a pleasure incident, brings Jimmy to present time, and then asks Jimmy what has happened during the session. Jimmy recites it and is pleased.

Later, in a private conference with the father, the auditor pointed out to him that "Go to bed" and "Take a bath," as commanded in the father's dominating voice might key in the "You're a big baby" circuit. Father supplied the information that every night it is a job to get Jimmy to bed. He tries to have him take a bath every other night. He finally has to force Jimmy by shouting the "Take a bath" and "Go to bed" orders as threats. Jimmy wets his bed almost every night. It was suggested that other means be used to get him to take a bath and go to bed, and that perhaps Mother's voice is not keyed in the circuit. It was also suggested that different words might do the trick, or that it might be best to allow Jimmy to go to bed when he likes. Father agreed to try.

At the auditor's next visit, one week later, Jimmy agrees to demonstrate for several people who are now interested. The auditor returns him to about the age of seven, after cautioning the spectators to be as quiet as possible.

Auditor: What are you doing?

Jimmy: *Playing with my dog, Pinky.*

Auditor: Where is this?

Jimmy: *In the back yard at Purcell Street.*

Auditor: What sort of day is it?

Jimmy: *Hot.*

Auditor: How old are you?

Jimmy: *Five.*

Auditor: What happens?

Jimmy: *I am feeding my dog.*

Auditor: And what is your age please?

Jimmy: *Five.*

Auditor: What year is it?

Jimmy: *1947.*

(Five is the wrong age, but the year and circumstances check. This incident is run several times and Jimmy is asked to go to an incident at the age of six.)

Auditor: What are you doing?

Jimmy: *I'm learning to ride my new bike.*

Auditor: Yes or no — do you have an accident?

Jimmy: *Yes.*

Auditor: Let's go to an earlier pleasure incident at about the age of four. *(Pause.)* How do you feel?

Jimmy: *Fine.*

Auditor: What are you doing? *(The auditor runs Jimmy through two other incidents, several times, and then brings him up to present time.)*

Auditor: Are you in present time?

Jimmy: *Yes.* (Eyes are still closed.)

Auditor: What do you see?

Jimmy: *I see the baby eating animal crackers.*

This astounded the observers, as the animal cracker box hadn't been given to the baby until after Jimmy was in reverie. Jimmy was then sent from the room with the explanation that information about this return in reverie would be given to him later. The auditor added that he wanted to encourage Jimmy's own views of the matter without having them influenced by the questions the observers might ask. Jimmy agreed.

The reason for not approaching the smash-up of the bicycle at this time—that the preclear was not prepared to face it—was given. Also given the observers was an explanation of the present time animal cracker scent—that the noises made by the animal cracker box and the baby were a translation into the visual perceptic by the boy's analytical mind. Further, even had the auditor thought it fantasy, extrasensory perception or just a guess, he would not have communicated the fact to the preclear, as this would have invalidated his sense of reality.

After the demonstration with Jimmy, the observers were

interested in trying Dianetics immediately. Six other persons were run through the experience of returning to incidents in their childhood. Judy's mother mentioned that Judy couldn't remember things that happened farther back than six months before.

Judy and her mother are separated from the father. Judy seems obviously affected by early arguments between Father and Mother. Later, when Judy came in and volunteered to demonstrate, the auditor returned her to an incident at the age of four.

Auditor: Where are you?

Jimmy: *In the field next door.*

Auditor: What's happening?

Judy: *I'm having my picture taken.*

Auditor: How do you feel?

Judy: *I'm mad.*

Auditor: What are you mad about?

Judy: *I don't know—I'm just mad.*

Auditor: Who's taking your picture?

Judy: *The man next door.*

Auditor: What does he say?

Judy: *"Come on, let's smile."*

Auditor: Do you?

Judy: *No.*

Auditor: What makes you mad?

Judy: *I don't know—I just am.*

(Auditor computes that finding out what made Judy mad may be restimulative to the mother, who is an observer. It may concern the father and mother, so the auditor does not try to find the origin of this feeling. After running this incident several times, Judy is sent to a more pleasant incident at the age of five.)

Judy: *My girlfriend is showing me her collection of dolls. She is rich.*

Auditor: What is her name?

Judy: *Barbara.*

Auditor: What happens now?

Judy: *Barbara goes out of the room. Her mother calls her.*

Auditor: What do you do?

Judy: *Stand and look at all the dolls. She has every kind.*

Auditor: Are you having fun?

Judy: *Yes.*

Auditor: And how old are you at this time?

Judy: *Five.*

Auditor: What next?

Judy: *Barbara comes back in.*

Auditor: What does she say?

Judy: *"I've got to do the dishes now."*

Auditor: What do you say?

Judy: *Do you have to do things when your parents say?*

Auditor: Does she answer?

Judy: *Yes.*

Auditor: What?

Judy: *"Yes"*

Auditor: And you—

Judy: *I say, "Oh."*

(This incident is related several times and then Judy is brought to present time. Judy's mother is pleased by the demonstration but risks invalidating data by talking about it in front of the child. For some reason, her mother insists on filling in: Judy was always mad at the man next door; would never smile when he was around. Also, she says Judy gets names wrong:

Barbara was another girlfriend, and the one with all the dolls was June. The auditor quickly changes the conversation by asking for another preclear to demonstrate.)

The next day the auditor resumed his sessions with Jimmy.

Auditor: Whom are you like in your family?

Jimmy: *Oh, I don't know.* (Shrugs)

Auditor: Are you like your father?

Jimmy: *No.*

Auditor: Mother?

Jimmy: *No.*

Auditor: Sister?

Jimmy: *No—not like her at all.*

Auditor: Did anyone ever say that you were just like your father, your mother, or anyone else?

Jimmy: *No.* (Shrugs) *No one said anything like that.*

Auditor: Who in your family wears glasses? *(Jimmy wears glasses for schoolwork.)*

Jimmy: *Father and Mother and my sister. All of them. Except the baby.*

Auditor: When did you first wear glasses?

Jimmy: *Last year.*

Auditor: When did you first notice you needed glasses?

Jimmy: *I was reading my school lessons at school and when I finished I looked up and couldn't see very well.*

Auditor: When was this?

Jimmy: *Last year.*

Auditor: All right, let's see about that. Make yourself comfortable on the bed. (Jimmy does.) Now it may be necessary to return to a moment where you are uncomfortable, have a pain or what is called a somatic. A somatic is a feeling of pain. By running through this somatic several times it will go away. In Dianetics it is necessary to return to this somatic and eliminate it, do away with it, so that we have greater pleasure in life. Are you willing to do this?

Jimmy: *Yes.*

Auditor: Remember, just be prepared to do what I ask and the somatic will go after we go over it several times. You will remember all that happens.

Jimmy: *Okay.*

Auditor: Return to the first time you thought you didn't see so well. *(Pause.)* What are you doing?

Jimmy: *I was in school.*

Auditor: What do you see?

Jimmy: *My teacher, Mr. Bidwell.*

Auditor: What is he saying?

Jimmy: *"Turn to the problems in your arithmetic book—page 46."*

Auditor: What happens?

Jimmy: *I do the problems.*

Auditor: Do you see the first problem?

Jimmy: *Yes.*

Auditor: Read it to me.

Jimmy: *I can't.*

Auditor: Maybe you can if you try. Read it to me. *(Jimmy reads the problem from visio recall.)*

Auditor: Do you have trouble with problems?

Jimmy: *No.*

Auditor: Are you good at arithmetic?

Jimmy: *Yes. That is, pretty good.*

Auditor: How about your eyes?

Jimmy: *When I finish the problems, I look up and don't see so very good.*

Auditor: Yes or no—is this the first time?

Jimmy: *No.*

Auditor: Let's return to the very first time this happens. *(Pause.)* What are you doing?

Jimmy: *I am reading my science lesson at school. I look up and I don't see so very good.*

Auditor: How old are you at this time?

Jimmy: *Nine.*

Auditor: Go through this incident again. *(The auditor has Jimmy read the science lesson from visio recall, but the content of the lesson seems to have nothing to do with his eyes.)*

Auditor: What happened three days before this science lesson?

Jimmy: *Nothing.*

Auditor: Let's return to three days before this time. *(Pause.)* What are you doing?

Jimmy: *Reading my science lesson.*

Auditor: Same one?

Jimmy: *No.*

Auditor: How are your eyes?

Jimmy: *Okay.*

Auditor: Anything happen that evening? Any quarrels?

Jimmy: *No.*

Auditor: All right, let's return to that other time, when you look up from the lesson and can't see so well. What do you do afterward, when you go home?

Jimmy: *Tell my mother.*

Auditor: What does she say?

Jimmy: *Maybe I'm reading too much. I ought to go to a doctor for a checkup.*

Auditor: How do you feel?

Jimmy: *Fine.*

Auditor: Let's go now to the incident needed to resolve the case. When I speak the letters from A to E and snap my fingers, you will be at the beginning of the incident. A-B-C-D-E. *(snap!)* What do you hear?

Jimmy: *I am reading my science lesson in school.*

Auditor: How old are you?

Jimmy: *Nine.*

Auditor: Let's return to the incident needed to resolve this case. When I recite the first five letters of the alphabet you will hear the first words of the incident. A-B-C-D-E. *(snap!)* What happens?

Jimmy: *I am in school, going over my science lesson.* (Jimmy goes through this again and the auditor tries another approach, reasoning that Jimmy does not understand what he means. The auditor wants to find out just how much Jimmy does understand.)

Auditor: Let's return to the first moment of conception. Return to the first moment of conception.

Jimmy: (Pauses.)

Auditor: Return to the first moment of conception. *(Jimmy starts through science lesson again. The problem here is what will Jimmy understand when the auditor is trying to enter an engram.)*

Auditor: Let's return to the first moment of discomfort, the very first moment of discomfort. Return to the first, very earliest moment of discomfort. *(Pause.)* What happens?

Jimmy: *My mother was spanking me.*

Auditor: How old are you?

Jimmy: *About a year and a half.*

Auditor: Yes or no—is this the first time you were ever spanked?

Jimmy: *Yes.*

Auditor: What does your mother say?

Jimmy: *Nothing.*

Auditor: Does anyone else say anything?

Jimmy: *No.*

Auditor: Does a neighbor speak to your mother?

Jimmy: *No.*

Auditor: Yes or no—are there any words in this incident?

Jimmy: *No.*

(The auditor risks invalidating data here by continuing to ask for words and phrases. He realizes, of course, or should if he knows his Dianetics, that there are engrams without verbal content.)

Auditor: How does it feel?

Jimmy: *Not so good.*

Auditor: What does your mother say?

Jimmy: *Nothing.*

Auditor: What do you say?

Jimmy: *I cry.*

Auditor: What happens then?

Jimmy: *Mother takes me in and puts me in the crib.*

Auditor: What do you do?

Jimmy: *I keep on crying for a little while.*

Auditor: Let's return to the beginning of the incident.

Jimmy: *My mother was spanking me.*

Auditor: What happens before your mother spanks you?

Jimmy: *I was reaching for something on the coffee table.*

Auditor: What does Mother say?

Jimmy: *"Don't touch that. If you do, I'll have to spank you and put you to bed."*

Auditor: Where are you?

Jimmy: *In the front room.*

Auditor: What are you reaching for?

Jimmy: (Pause.) *A . . . an ash tray.*

Auditor: What happens?

Jimmy: *My mother picks me up and spanks me.*

Auditor: What does she say?

Jimmy: *Nothing.*

Auditor: Can you feel the spanking?

Jimmy: *Yes.* (Jimmy's body position shows that he is feeling pain.)

Auditor: Is it too painful?

Jimmy: *No.*

Auditor: What happens then?

Jimmy: *My mother takes me in the bedroom and puts me in the crib.* (By the fourth time through this incident the somatic is reduced.)

Auditor: How do you feel? Shall we go on?

Jimmy: *Fine. Okay.*

Auditor: Now, let's return to way before you were born, to the first moment you were aware. Return to way before you were born. When I go from A to E and snap my fingers you will hear the first words. A-B-C-D-E. *(snap!)* What do you hear?

Jimmy: *Nothing.*

Auditor: When I read from A to E you will hear the first words. A-B-C-D-E. *(snap!)* What do you hear?

Jimmy: *Nothing.*

Auditor: What happens?

Jimmy: *My mother was out walking. She walks a couple of blocks and turns around and comes home.*

Auditor: Pick it up at the beginning and go through it again.

Jimmy: *My mother was out walking.*

Auditor: What do you hear?

Jimmy: *Cars going by.*

Auditor: What does your mother say?

Jimmy: *Nothing.*

Auditor: What do you see?

Jimmy: *Nothing.*

Auditor: How old are you?

Jimmy: *Eight.*

Auditor: Yes or no, is it eight days?

Jimmy: *Yes.*

Auditor: Continue.

Jimmy: *Mother walks a couple of blocks, turns around and comes home.*

Auditor: How do you feel? Is there any discomfort?

Jimmy: *Yes, all over my body.*

Auditor: Where are you?

Jimmy: *In my mother's stomach.*

Auditor: Start at the beginning.

Jimmy: *My mother was out walking.*

Auditor: What happens first? Let's go back ten minutes before this. What is happening?

Jimmy: *I'm asleep. My mother walks down the steps and up the block.*

Auditor: Just where do you wake up?

Jimmy: *Just as she steps down the bottom step.*

Auditor: Just as she steps down the bottom step?

Jimmy: *Yes.*

Auditor: Then?

Jimmy: *She walks up the street.*

Auditor: What do you hear?

Jimmy: *Cars going by.*

Auditor: Anything else?

Jimmy: *My mother's footsteps.*

Auditor: How do you feel?

Jimmy: *Not too bad.*

Auditor: What happens next?

Jimmy: *Mother turns around and walks home.*

Auditor: What happens when she gets home?

Jimmy: *She walks up the steps into the house.*

Auditor: How many steps?

Jimmy: (Pauses and counts steps.) *One, two, three, four. Four.*

Auditor: What do you see?

Jimmy: *Nothing.* (A confirmation: there is no visio in the prenatal period, though there are other perceptics.)

Auditor: Can you hear the door slam?

Jimmy: *Yes.*

Auditor: What does your mother do then?

Jimmy: *She sits down.*

Auditor: What do you do?

Jimmy: *I go to sleep.* (On the fourth run through the complete incident the discomfort somatic reduces. At the twelfth run the sonic content remains, although perhaps not as intense as before. Jimmy seems relaxed, refreshed and pleased. A pleasure incident is run and then Jimmy is asked to come to present time.)

Auditor: What's your age now?

Jimmy: *I'm ten years old.*

Auditor: You may open your eyes.

Jimmy: (Opens his eyes.) *They're not the same as before.*

Auditor: What's not the same?

Jimmy: *My eyes. I can see. The other times I had trouble seeing when I opened them.*

Auditor: Good. How do you feel otherwise?

Jimmy: *Good.*

Auditor: How'd you like it?

Jimmy: *Fine. I didn't understand those long words in the middle.*

Auditor: Oh? Well, sometimes I use words in my language that mean things you don't know in your language. If I ever use a word you don't know, ask me and I'll explain it in your language. You probably already know what it means. What were the words? Do you mean *conception?*

Jimmy: *Yes.*

Auditor: Conception is the meeting of the father's cells with the mother's cells before they become a baby. You know it in those words, don't you?

Jimmy: *Yes.*

Auditor: And somatic? Somatic means pain. Pain—somatic. Understand?

Jimmy: *Yes.*

Auditor: Any others?

Jimmy: *No.*

Auditor: Ask me if you think of any. Okay?

Jimmy: *Yes.*

Auditor: Do you remember what happened?

Jimmy: *Yes, you worked with my eyes and my mother was out walking before I was a baby.*

Auditor: Have you wet the bed lately?

Jimmy: *Just once. It was last night.*

This session lasted one hour and twenty minutes, and it was now time for supper. Jimmy was pleased enough to tell his parents something about the session.

As to the preclear's statement about his eyes feeling better, we may assume that any improvement in this respect was due to a general release of tension, since the engram contacted apparently contained no material which could be constructed to be directly affecting Jimmy's eyes.

10

Some Cases
in Point

10

Some Cases in Point

C-211:

Child's Name: Richard Jackson, ("Dickey")

Age: 7

Father's Name: Charles

Mother's Name: Emma

Grandmother: "Bamma"

Mother's Complaint: "I can't make him mind."

Accidents: Auto accident age five, several stitches taken in left arm, no anesthetic administered.

Chronic Somatics: Colds, sore throat.

Dramatizations: Baby talk.

When Dickey first came to the Foundation for processing, he was obviously a serious behavior problem. He refused to play with other children, would kick at them and try to scratch their faces. He ran wildly around the playroom, opening doors and trying to get out. Upon opening the door leading to the outdoor play yard, he quickly closed it again. There were other children out there.

Physically he had a clean bill of health from the family doctor, although colds and sore throat were chronic complaints. He had a very limited vocabulary, his speech was poor, and he indulged almost exclusively in "baby talk." There was no physical defect of vocal cords or tongue.

According to his mother he was constantly hungry, but would eat only meat and soup at home, and at school only soup or milk. He constantly refused sandwiches, even though they contained meat. In answer to the auditor's question as to what foods he preferred, Dickey answered, "No!"

Several phrases were highly recurrent. "No" seemed to be his favorite and was said at any irrelevant moment during a conversation. "I don't know!" vehemently expressed for no apparent reason during conversations, and "goodbye" every few sentences were two others. Questioning (straight line memory) about these phrases brought an instant reaction of fear, and even to the time of this writing no definite information on actual incidents containing them has been gained.

Progress was very slow for Dickey during the first fifteen sessions. He refused to cooperate with the auditor in any way. He did not cry. Rather, there was an outward expression of defiance, as though he would accept any punishment rather than show tears. He would at times be sullen and silent, and others scream and kick. When asked to string beads, play with blocks or lie down and close his eyes, he would throw the beads and blocks at the windows, and lie down and keep his eyes very wide open.

Finally, at the sixteenth session, the auditor noted a distinct change. When asked to lie down and close his eyes, Dickey said, "All right. For a little while." From that time through the fiftieth hour of processing he became more and more cooperative in every way.

His perceptics seem to be good. He can describe rooms, the people who were in them and what they did. He can often see himself in the room, and does not like the little boy he sees. He now cooperates in processing, and rather enjoys it as a game between himself and the auditor, for whom he has developed a deep affinity. When asked questions he gives limited answers, but shows signs of developing initiative in elaboration.

The noticeable progress which has taken place at this writing is a definite improvement in behavior. His speech has improved considerably, and the use of baby talk has diminished to almost nil. He has taken a liking to certain other children, and gets along famously with one little boy in particular. When *asked* to do something he will carry it out happily and willingly. Instead of throwing his blocks, he constructs imaginary houses, walls and various objects inside them. He strings beads in color patterns, vying with the other children for neatness in so doing.

In general, he now participates well in all the children's activities.

Total hours of processing to date: Fifty-six hours.

C-173:

Child's Name: Stanley Vinyl, ("Stan")

Age: 9

Father's Name: Warren

Mother's Name: Cora

Grandmother's Name: "Granny"

Sister: Sally

Medical Data: Three days old, lung collapsed; pneumonia. Seven weeks, hernia. One and a half years, convulsions, increasingly worse, continuing until three and a half years of age. Phenobarbital[1] prescribed by pediatrician; still using it. Three and a half years, hernia reappeared; operation on hernia. Five years, virus infection. Major convulsion, hospitalized, oxygen and hypodermics. Violent attack of gastritis.[2] Six years, convulsion. Seven years, fell and cut head open, several stitches, no anesthetic. Hit by baseball bat same year, breaking glasses and raising welt under right eye. Eight years, convulsion. Nine years, hit by automobile, bruised and shaken.

Stanley lives with his mother, father, sister, grandfather, a monologist grandmother and an uncle. The father stutters when excited, and thinks the mother is much too "soft" with Stan. Grandfather often speaks in his native tongue to Grandmother.

Mother's punishment of Stan consists of a strapping with Father's belt, or a razor strop industriously and frequently applied. Milder punishments take the form of forbidding him to watch television, or tying him to a table leg for extended periods. Father enforces his demands for obedience with an occasional slap across Stan's mouth.

All the adults in the family carry on frequent free-for-all

---

1. **phenobarbital:** a white crystalline powder used as a sedative, a hypnotic and as an antispasmodic in epilepsy.

2. **gastritis:** inflammation of the stomach, especially of its mucous membrane.

arguments, talking about the children as though they were not present. The arguments have occasionally wound up with irate neighbors demanding peace and quiet, and with the police at the door.

The mother is neurotically concerned about the physical health of the entire family, and is constantly stating that neither Sally nor Stan likes to be away from her.

When Stan first appeared for processing, his speech was very difficult to understand. He tried desperately to talk, but stuttered badly. He had a fear bordering on terror when about to be left alone, or in the company of only other children. He had to have an adult around at all times. He showed extreme aggression toward other children, fighting continually by scratching, biting and kicking.

The following list of phrases have been discovered both in Stan's processing and from observation. Some of the valences are known and are accordingly indicated, but many are not clear even in Stan's own memory bank, being confused with one another.

"I want to eat breakfast." (Uncle)

"I want to ask a question before we go any further."

"Will you come here?" (Father, Mother; prenatal call-back)

"Goodbye! I'm going to leave you."

"I'm a prisoner." (Mother)

"Will you get out of here, you wild fool?" (Mother)

"Be a good boy." (All adults)

"Be a good boy or I'll hit you across the neck." (Uncle)

"I'll kick you in the teeth." (Father)

"I'll knock all your teeth out." (Father)

"Is that clear?"

"Will you leave me alone?" (Mother)

"I'll give you just one more chance." (Mother)

"Just a minute now, just a minute." (Mother)

"Stop a minute." (Mother)

"I want to ask just one question."

"Hold everything six months."

"Christmas is coming up."

"Period!"

"Hold everything!"

(The auditor's computation thus far was: Everything means the same as nothing, which means zero. Nothing means no hat, no coat, no shoes, no socks, no pants, no clothes, no food, no fish, no horse, no office.)

"Where do we go from here?"

"Come here, you stupid fool." (Grandfather)

"Nothing happened."

"No good."

During processing, Stan shows a fair ability to return to specific incidents; however, as soon as he contacts a few perceptics and begins to approach the period of physical or emotional pain, he reverts to "make-believe." The prenatal period is easily contacted, Stan apparently being able to get both perceptics and somatics. These somatics can be run only once or twice, then he begins to avoid them.

He has many phrases in his bank that command him either directly or indirectly to keep quiet or to keep his mouth shut. Late-life incidents pertaining to his speech difficulty contain phrases such as, "I'll knock your teeth out" and "I'll tear your tongue out." Stan habitually hides his teeth behind his lips and holds his tongue withdrawn, hindering his pronunciation of *L's* and *F's*.

Stan has continually evidenced a prenatal restimulation that causes him to jump from valence to valence, always taking a highly aggressive role. The phrases contacted in the prenatal area (about six months according to flash) contain computations that nothing is everything, and that nothing is zero; nothing implies no clothes, no food, no office, and just "no." Nothing is also a person, the identity of whom is not yet known.

Some special techniques have been used on Stan. One of the most successful consists of telling him that he is about to be left alone; that the auditor will be back right away. It is explained to him that the purpose of this action is to help him remember how he felt on the other occasions when he was left alone. He understands, has always broken into tears upon such restimulation, and has carried the tears back to instances when his mother and his grandmother had left him.

In processing Stan, several different chains were begun in succession and a continual switch from chain to chain was carried out. The reason for this procedure was that too much emphasis on grief or pain seemed to antagonize him and make him reluctant to continue processing. The same grief incident was contacted at four different sessions, and the last time contacted the restimulation from being left alone carried him back into the original incident and some degree of reduction was accomplished. The restimulation was then run out as a lock.

If Stan is allowed to suggest the incident to which he wants to return, he supplies the skeleton of its beginning, then will make up a fanciful tale based on it in which everything turns out all right. When the auditor directs him to a specific incident or type of incident, he seems to give a fairly straight report.

At times processing is impeded by his dramatizations. One session was constantly interrupted by a phrase from a violent prenatal that was unavailable: "Before we go any further, I'd like to ask you a question." When he was allowed to ask the question (which turned out to be "Where do we go next?"), processing continued.

The noticeable progress has been a tremendous improvement in speech, cooperation with the auditor and in playing with other children.

Total hours of processing to date: Twenty-five hours; continuing.

C-103:

Name: Robert Williams, ("Bobby")

Age: 10

Father's Name: Perry

Mother's Name: Celia

Grandmother: Edith

Aunts: "Dilly"; Esther

Uncle: Fred

Illnesses: Digestive upsets, skin disease. Placed in heat crib in infancy. Acidosis,[3] dehydrated, excessive urination and salivation.

Chronic Somatics: Colds, nose drainages.

Dramatizations: Tantrum; crying spells.

Overt Behavior: Fluttering of eyelids, closing of eyes, tensing of muscles, clenching of hands. Constant flipping of any object held in hands. Sits with books and turns pages for hours at a time. Excellent musical memory, rhythm and coordination. Manual dexterity good. Constant dramatization of incidents happening at home. Changes valences rapidly, and speaks of himself in third person.

Observations: Will not learn to read. Completely breaks down any attempt at formal education. Speech, excellent. Words used, very advanced for his age. Completely uncontrollable. Very little touch with reality. Computation that everything equals everything else.

---

3. **acidosis:** a harmful condition in which the blood and tissues are less alkaline than is normal.

Previous Professional Diagnoses: Numerous speculations have come from various sources in the past, i.e., mentally retarded, thyroid[4] imbalance, encephalitis[5] and schizoid.

In the words of the boy's Dianetic auditor, "Bobby seems to be multivalent and in synthesis with an 'I' that is very much disliked by a swarm of anti-Bobby demons,[6] which have the analyzer in a very effective straitjacket."

Bobby has many overt symptoms of his maladjustments: visio hallucinations, contortions, stiffening of muscles, crying spells, laughing jags,[7] etc. When starting sessions he usually says, "Don't want to play remembering," but once the session has begun, he is very quiet and will close his eyes and cooperate. However, in returning to phrases and incidents he seems to be stuck at about the age of five in a residential school he attended, to which he refers as "The Rhynes."

Responses to questioning are rather irrational, with no visible relationship between sentences. It always "happened at The Rhynes" or "Nance said it." So far there is no indication as who "Nance" might be.

Bobby does not dramatize in processing as he does in present time. He does not run engrams because he cannot get

---

4. **thyroid:** concerning the thyroid gland, an important ductless gland in the neck of vertebrates, near the larynx and upper windpipe, that affects growth and metabolism.

5. **encephalitis:** inflammation of the brain caused by injury, infection, poison or other agent. Sleeping sickness is one kind of encephalitis.

6. **demons:** mechanical mechanisms set up by an engram which take over a portion of the analyzer and act as individual beings. A bonafide demon is one who gives thoughts voice or echoes the spoken word interiorly or who gives all sorts of complicated advice like a real, live voice exteriorly.

7. **jags:** a period of unrestrained indulgence in an activity; spree; binge.

more than one phrase at a time. The succeeding phrases are always related to something other than the beginning phrase. He has various somatics, both in and out of processing, and readily tells where it hurts by pointing to various parts of his body.

Bobby's mother was about thirty-five at the time of pregnancy, and was advised by her husband, friends and family to consider abortion. She declares that she did not (?). During pregnancy she went to a psychologist whose therapy consisted of shouting "dirty" words at her "in order to get you over your squeamishness."

The father is evidently a "control" case, a man who is dramatically "head of the house." He wants to know nothing about Dianetics or, to use his words, "I'd probably stop the damned thing if I knew what was going on." He appears in Bobby's bank both as an ally and as an antagonist. Bobby frequently dramatizes Father's verbalizations.

Bobby is hindered in processing by unusual restimulation at home. Each session must be begun with running locks incurred in association with his family during the interval since the previous session. The parents have grudgingly attended several special lectures given by the auditor, and the mother has read *Dianetics: The Modern Science of Mental Health*. In spite of this attempt at educating the parents, the ideal solution in Bobby's case while processing continues would be a residential school.

The following is a record of a directed monologue by Bobby Williams:

Bobby: *Good means I'm good. Good means something good. It doesn't mean candy, it means blocks. It's something I do. I build trains. The train's something. Something to go woo-woo. I never been on one.*

Auditor: Who was on the train, Bobby?

Bobby: *Someone was. I went. Well . . . it was off the train and I was at The Rhynes. I'm the at The Rhynes now. It's a locomotive. It's the first car on the train. That's the car that pulls all the other cars. Locomotive. Locomotive goes . . . goes somewhere . . . goes to the somewhere. Somewhere is.*

Auditor: Is it dark inside?

Bobby: *Yes, it feels good.*

Auditor: Who says it?

Bobby: *Celia says it feels good, it hurts.*

Auditor: Is there a difference between hurting and feeling good?

Bobby: *There is.*

Auditor: Do you like to get hurt?

Bobby: *Don't wanna get hurt. It was wet. It wasn't wet, it was dry. It's good when it's wet. It's good and wet. It's dark. Eyes are closed. It's pushing here.* (Points to spot on abdomen.)

Auditor: Where else is it pushing?

Bobby: *All over, it's pushing all over. It hurts. I'm asleep.*

Auditor: What would happen if you wake up?

Bobby: *Something will happen.*

Auditor: Is something good or bad?

Bobby: *It's good. Something would happen* (begins to cry). *Something good will happen* (cries again). *Something's the best thing that can happen. Something's the best thing that can happen. Something's the best thing that can happen. Something's the best thing that can happen.*

Auditor: What's another word for something?

Bobby: *Something. Something. Something. Something. Isn't that something? Isn't that something? Isn't that something? Isn't that something?*

Auditor: Is that a good sentence?

Bobby: *Yes. Play's a good sentence. That's a good sentence. Feels . . . good. It feels good. I play. I worked.*

Auditor: What comes right before that?

Bobby: *Something comes right after that. Something comes before that. It's blocks. It's not good for eating. Something's good for eating.*

Auditor: What are blocks for?

Bobby: *Blocks are good blocks. Blocks are good for eating. Blocks are something. Blocks are made out of not wood.*

Auditor: What are boys made of?

Bobby: *Boys are made of wood.*

Auditor: What are boys' heads made of?

Bobby: *My head is made of wood. I believe it.*

Auditor: What's wood?

Bobby: *Something's wood. Would you please make me out of wood? Wood. Wood. Wood. Wood.*

Auditor: Next?

Bobby: *I played. Would you please play with those blocks? Would you, please? That makes him not work.*

Auditor: Are you him?

Bobby: *I'm not him. I don't know what him is. He's him. Will you please play with those blocks? I told him not to, please.*

Auditor: Did you learn that at The Rhynes?

Bobby: *Yes. Wanna work. Please play. I worked. Will you please play with those blocks? Will you please play with those blocks? Will you please play with those blocks? Will you please play with those blocks?*

Auditor: What did they give you if you played with blocks?

Bobby: *They'd say . . . (silence).*

Auditor: What did they give you if you played with blocks?

Bobby: *They give him something.*

Auditor: What's another word for something?

Bobby: *It's not candy. It's not candy. It's not candy. It's not candy. They say they'd give him candy. They gave him candy. It was at The Rhynes. The Rhynes are something. It's good.*

Auditor: What's good?

Bobby: *Something's good. I'm not gonna have it, I'm not.*

Auditor: What is something?

Bobby: *It's wood. It's not wood. I'm playing.*

Auditor: Who's playing?

Bobby: *I'm playing with The Rhynes. I'm playing with something. It's a train.*

Auditor: What is a train?

Bobby: *Something is a train.*

Auditor: Is training like learning?

Bobby: *It's training. It goes choo-choo-choo.*

Auditor: Did anyone ever train you to do something?

Bobby: *Someone did.*

The computations that are damaging in a preclear's bank depend on the extent of seeming "similarity" between events that actually are not similar. Thus, when one is trying to trace down a computation, he might do well to ask for the "sameness" in things, tracing down close and remote connections. The closest identifications between any two events are in most instances the strongest aberrative factors.

Here follows a transcript of a session with Bobby Williams, showing an application of this technique, the object of which was to discover chains of phrases that are to him the same.

Auditor: What word is the same as dead?

Bobby: *Something is the same as dead. Something is dangerous.*

Auditor: What is the same as dangerous?

Bobby: *Bobby went in hell.*

Auditor: What's the same as Bobby went in hell?

Bobby: *Something is the same as go to hell.* (Puts hand over mouth) *I'll tell what the same is.*

Auditor: What's the same as go to hell?

Bobby: *Go to hell is go to hell.*

Auditor: What word is the same as dead?

Bobby: *Something's the same. Something's the same. Something's the same. Something's the same. Go to hell.*

Auditor: What is the same thing as go to hell?

Bobby: *Have you done the same?*

Auditor: Say more.

Bobby: (Silence)

Auditor: What is the same thing as dangerous?

Bobby: *Something is go to hell.*

Auditor: What is the same thing as go to hell?

Bobby: *Something is.*

Auditor: What is go to hell?

Bobby: *Aaa-ha-ha!*

Auditor: Is that crying?

Bobby: (No response)

Auditor: What's the same as go to hell?

Bobby: (No response)

Auditor: What person is go to hell?

Bobby: *Something is go to hell.*

Auditor: What is hell?

Bobby: *Hell's go to hell: Wanta say canceled. He will, he'll say it.*

Auditor: What is the same as hell?

Bobby: *Something is the same as hell. It is. Go to hell.*

Auditor: What is almost the same as hell?

Bobby: (Smells hand)

Auditor: Is it *smell?*

Bobby: *Yes.*

Auditor: Is smell the same as hell? Yes or no?

Bobby: *Yes.*

Auditor: Is town the same as hell?

Bobby: *Yes. Have you done the same, then we'll say canceled.*

Somewhat later, following the end of the session, this question was asked: "Flash answer, Bobby. Yes or no?" *(snap!)*

"Yes!"

One can notice definite though restricted computations here. The conclusion would seem to be that the most immediate threat to Bobby's survival is "something" connected with an early chain in which Mother had said something like "Go to hell, it's too dangerous, I might die." Or perhaps the ideas of danger and death are connected to the mother by an attempted abortion chain with phrases about hell and damnation or just plain "Oh, hell" in it. From talks with the mother, it seems probable that an AA chain, or at least talk about abortion, exists in Bobby's banks.

The progress in this case has been fairly good, considering the very high emotional state in which Bobby usually appears for processing. As mentioned before, it would help matters considerably if Bobby could be removed from his home environment and its accompanying restimulation.

His tantrums are almost completely gone, occurring only at very extended intervals. Crying spells have decreased. He has more awareness and interest in things around him, and enjoys doing specified tasks. He seems to differentiate between things more realistically.

Total hours of processing to date: Twenty-five hours; continuing.

C-27:

Child's Name: Marie, ("Mame")

Age: 13

Father's Name: Clarence

Mother's Name: Peggy

Grandmother: Mater

Brother: Bobbie

Accidents: Fell from tree, age five. Broke arm, set without anesthetic. Slipped on pavement, age nine. Knocked out by blow on back of head.

Medical-Dental Record: Tooth pulled, age seven, nitrous oxide gas. Tonsillectomy, age nine, ether anesthetic.

Chronic Somatics: Constant sore throat, colds. Headaches causing fainting spells.

Marie was brought in for processing, not because she was an overt behavior problem, but because she seemed to be backward in studies and in her association with other children. There was no apparent explanation for this, since previous consultations with teachers and parents had established that she had a very high intelligence for her age.

She was very cooperative with the auditor from the first session. Her perceptics were good, and she returned readily and willingly to past incidents when requested to do so by the auditor. She would follow a chain down to the prenatal basic, run out the basic with little urging by the auditor, and then come up to present time by herself, saying, "This was fun. I'll come back again tomorrow and we'll do some more."

One of the engrams which was contacted in later processing was that of an exodontistry at the age of seven. The improvement in her studies and association with children her own age showed a remarkable improvement following the running of the nitrous-oxide engram.

Following is a word-by-word account of a portion of the processing session in which she contacted the dentist's office:

Marie: *Time tooth pulled . . . I can't get back . . . thought I was dying but couldn't get back. My teeth could drop out and I'd never have that again.*

Auditor: Tell me about it.

Marie: *The nurse puts the thing over my nose . . . "Relax honey. That's the girl . . . . All right, doctor, go ahead!" My eyes, presses on my eyes . . . Don't feel pain but it pulls and I can't tell him . . . . Jerks my head . . . No fighting . . . Don't know where I am . . . But I've got to*

get back . . . Dr. Penn says, "That's really a big one."
Then the nurse says, "It's out, it's all over. It's out. Put
your head over here and spit."

Auditor: And then what happens?

Marie: *I had an awful struggle to get back . . . . It was all*
red . . . . Never black, always red and orange . . . .
That stuff's no good.

Auditor: Continue, please.

Marie: (Silence)

Auditor: Is something holding you?

Marie: *Yes. He says, "Here, you can hold it." He gives me the*
tooth to take home. I go home with Bobbie.

Auditor: Let's return again to where you are sitting down in
the chair. Were you frightened?

Marie: *Nervous about going in . . . . The nurse had been—she*
puts the thing over my nose, and I breathe . . . . Feel her
lift my eyelids up . . . . She says, "All right, doctor."
My head starts to spin . . . . I feel that red, it keeps
pulling my head over to this side. (indicates by inclin-
ing head to right) *I can't get back . . . . I don't get*
back . . . . I can't get back . . . (excited, frantic) *It's all*
over . . . . It sure was a big one . . . . Gee, I'll never
take that stuff anymore . . . . Closest I ever came to
dying. . . . (Yawn, yawn)

Auditor: Let's start once more with the nurse adjusting the
mask.

Marie: *I can hear her, and she lifts my eyes and says, "All right, doctor." I think he can't do it yet, but I can't do anything about it . . . . Hear a sound . . . Things rattle, pliers and things . . . Starts to pull my head . . . . I didn't think I'd have to get back . . . . I didn't think I'd get back . . . . I can't get back . . . . They say something . . . . "You're all right, honey, just spit over in here." I look out the window and see our kitchen, then I know I'm back . . . .*

Auditor: Continue, Marie.

Marie: *I'll never do it again . . . . Bobbie takes me home . . . After I pay my money . . .*

Auditor: Let's repeat the entire incident once more. See if you can hear anything else this time, and if you can feel the chair you are sitting in, and the lights . . .

Marie: *Nurse puts it over my nose . . . . Feels cold . . . . Oh! I jump out and see myself sitting there instead of feeling anything.*

Auditor: Does anyone speak at this point?

Marie: *The nurse. She says, "She's out now."*

Auditor: May we continue now?

Marie: *I'm all mixed up . . . . I get up out of the chair . . . . She gives me a cup of water to rinse my mouth out with . . . . Takes things off my neck . . . . I ask her how much, she says four dollars . . . . I pay and wait in the waiting room . . . . Go downstairs with Bobbie . . . . Across street. . . . (Yawn, yawn, yawn)*

Auditor: Let's begin from the beginning, Marie. Start from . . .

Marie: (Expressing exasperation) *She puts it over my nose . . . . My chest heaves, I see red . . . . My hands on the arms of the chair . . . . She lifts my eyelids . . . . I wish she'd keep her damned hands out of my eyes . . . . He pulls my head over and over . . . . Spit in the thing . . . . She takes the thing off my neck . . . . Get purse and give her money . . . . Down hall, down stairs . . .*

Auditor: Let's run over it again . . .

Marie: (Interrupts) *I start to breathe deeply, head starts to feel funny, I close my eyes . . . . She tries to open them, lifts up the lid . . . . "All right, doctor . . . " I know it's not all right . . . I can still feel. Starts to pull my head, strong . . . I fight to get back . . . . Got to get back . . .* (Face contorted, struggling muscularly) *Just thinking about it's got my tooth to aching up here . . .* (Points to molar.)

Auditor: Please repeat from the beginning, Marie. Let's see if you can hear everything that goes on . . .

Marie: (Boredom) *Oh, my head hurts . . . . Do I have to do it again? Must I do it again. The nurse puts the thing over my nose, pulls up my eyelids and says, "All right, doctor . . . " I feel funny . . . . I can't do anything about it. I see redness . . . . He jerks my head . . . . I got to get back.* (Repeats phrase nine times, breathing very heavily.) *Finally I can open my eyes. She tells me to spit . . . . I see the water running in the fountain.* (Yawn) *I pay him . . . . Get out . . . . Go to wrong door. Nurse says, "You're all mixed up, honey."*

(Laughs heartily.) *So that's why I'm all mixed up!* (More laughter.) *I pay her. Go out . . . Bobbie helps me down . . . . Home . . .*

Auditor: Let's go over it once more, Marie.

Marie: *Gee, it's hard to do* (Sigh) *it . . . I just about know it by heart now . . . . She puts it over my nose . . . . Feel her press her fingers on eyes . . . . "All right, doctor" . . . I know it's not all right . . . . I'm glad when I see our house across the street . . . .*

Auditor: Once more, Marie, please.

Marie: *Oh, gosh!* (Sigh) *I wish I'd never even mentioned it! Oh, all right! She puts the thing over my nose . . . . She's in back of me . . . . Seems like a long time . . . . Puts her fingers up and pokes my eyes . . . . See red . . . "All right, doctor" . . . I'm not supposed to hear this, but I hear it* (Sigh) *I hear a sound . . . . An awful crack . . . Oh, Lord! Probably my tooth coming out . . . Breaks it and leaves a hunk in there . . . . Pulls like the dickens . . . . Says, "Sure is a tough one." Gosh, this tooth right here hurts* (Points to molar again.) *. . . Give him his darned four bucks and go home . . . . Probably broke his arm . . . . Rough . . . Enough trouble without going to a dentist.* (Sigh, yawn)

Auditor: Repeat this incident once more, please.

Marie: *Oh! You got a grudge against me, or something?* (Extreme exasperation) *Of all the ways to get even with a person . . . Sending them to a dentist . . . All right. She puts it over and I breathe . . . . Pokes her old finger in my eyeballs . . . . He goes ahead . . . . He pulls my* *head off . . . . I think I'm dying and try to get back.*

Auditor: *(After a few minutes of silence)* Once more, Marie.

Marie: *I'm going to bite you in a minute!* (Anger) *She puts the thing over my nose.* (Laughter) *Lifts up the peepers.* (Hearty laughter, auditor joining in.) *"All right, doctor." I see red . . . . I see it in both meanings!* (Laughter again.) *I finally come out of it safe and sound . . . . I never did like a dentist and you make me stay there so long . . .*

Auditor: Where are you now?

Marie: *Here, in the room, with you. I'm thirteen and it's Tuesday.* (Breaks into laughter). *Beat you to it that time!*

At this point she seemed to be happier and more cheerful than at any time the auditor had seen her. There was but one more session following, and then her mother called to say that they were so pleased with Marie that they didn't think she needed any more processing right then.

Eight months later she was among the top four in her classes, and very active in dramatics and sports. Her mother reported that to her knowledge Marie had not had a cold since she had left off processing.

Auditor's Computation: The phrase of the nurse, "You're all mixed up, honey," might well have caused her considerable trouble in her schoolwork. Chances are this phrase was keyed in by someone who resembled the nurse, which thereafter made her studies more difficult.

Total hours of processing: Fifteen hours.

11

A Look Ahead

11

A Look Ahead

In our hands lies the future of the world, for as we train our children we shape in them the pattern of things to come. We, who are filled with the aberrations inherited from our parents, heretofore could only be resigned to pass on these aberrations to our children in ever-increasing intensity. 'Round and 'round it has gone, and where it might stop nobody has known.

But now Dianetics has come to break the spiral. And for every father or mother interested in Dianetics, the big question is, "What can I do for my children?"

Let us consider how to begin this business of Child Dianetics. One of the most important tools we can use is observation. What are your child's aberrations? What are his push-buttons?[1] From whom did the child acquire that peculiar behavior? Why does she get so many colds? Why does he seem to get edgy and start crying when we try to hurry him? Why won't she drink milk or eat crackers? Why? Every item of the

---

1. **push-buttons:** items, words, phrases, subjects or areas that are easily restimulatable in an individual by the words or actions of other people, and which cause him discomfort, embarrassment or upset, or make him laugh uncontrollably.

child's conduct should be observed and correlation made of these items with the parents' own cases. Look at yourselves! Be aware of your own case, keep thorough notes on your own processing. By doing so, you will soon have the key to the child's problem.

As an example, here is the experience the parents of one child had. Their daughter, age five, had a very bad night with bronchial trouble; and the whole winter following suffered a succession of colds. A curious fact that eventually led to an explanation was that she would allow her parents to put Mentholatum[2] in her nose but was very much opposed to Vaseline.[3] One night the problem was solved. Mother, during processing, ran her daughter's birth. Right from the heart of the incident came the phrase, "I can't breathe. I'm all stopped up." This phrase was repeated a number of times during the birth. A phrase that regularly accompanied the first was, "Can't I have some Mentholatum for my nose?" The nurse replied, "Here is some Vaseline; it's all we have." The mother answered, "I don't want Vaseline, I want Mentholatum!"

Since this discovery the parents have exercised care not to use the phrase, "I can't breathe; I'm all stopped up." Result? Practically no colds and no repetition of the bronchial condition. What about the Vaseline? That is now called petroleum jelly, and the child uses it when necessary.

The principles explained in this book may go a long way toward making yours an optimum family. But these principles must be mastered. This can be done only by constant practice, observation and study.

---

2. **Mentholatum:** a brand name for a mentholated salve used as a chest rub for colds or flu.

3. **Vaseline:** a brand name for a petroleum jelly product.

If you have a number of friends with children and an interest in Dianetics, or an interest in improving their family relationships, you may organize a study group. For best results, this group should include not more than ten couples. Discussion must necessarily be more and more restricted as the group's size increases. Where the group grows unwieldy, there is less time for consideration of the individual problems of those who compose it.

Step One, the beginning of such a program, is simple. If you have children you have problems. The first step is to use the material in this book as a basis for discussion supervised by a group discussion leader. The leader should be replaced from time to time, to provide fresh points of view. From the discussion a solid understanding of the basic principles of Dianetics and Child Dianetics may be gained.

Step Two, which should form a portion of every program from the first one on, is a presentation by each member of some of the specific personal problems with children. The group then discusses each problem in an attempt to help the parent discover the Dianetic solution.

Step Three is the testing of these solutions in the home by every group member whose problem is similar.

Step Four, at subsequent meetings, is a discussion of the practical applications of the solutions suggested, and an evaluation of the results with a view to striving for constant improvement of the techniques.

Step Five is a report to the Foundation of what has been accomplished each time a definite workable technique is evolved.

Here are a few subjects you will find of real value in building stronger families:

Family Relations: What could be more important in family relations than a complete understanding of the affinity, reality and communication triangle?[4] This is perhaps the most important point for your group study. What do the terms mean to each individual? What are ARC breaks and what do they do? How can you run them out of yourselves and your children? How do these principles as symbolized by the triangle apply in all interpersonal situations?

Remember that the principles set forth in this book are stepping stones toward larger discoveries. Dianetics is a very new science. It will progress by the research of all who consistently apply it. After each group discussion, set up a test program for your homes. Keep notes on your trials and errors. Bring the results to future meetings for further evaluations. Keep a group record of the correlated material.

Discipline: Here is a crucial subject, one that Dianetics tends to highlight. It gives the parents who have over-disciplined their children a definite feeling of guilt. "Is it I who has laid in my child's aberrations? Here is my control circuit—I have laid it into my child!" It is futile to castigate[5] oneself for not knowing about Dianetics before it was made available to the public. Console yourself with the fact that everybody else was guilty of the same pre-Dianetic sins against posterity, and that within our lifetime there is yet the opportunity to give the future a new lease on

---

4. **affinity, reality and communication triangle:** a triangle which is a symbol of the fact that affinity, reality and communication act together as a whole entity and that one of them cannot be considered unless the other two are also taken into account. Without affinity there is no reality or communication. Without reality or some agreement, affinity and communication are absent. Without communication there can be no affinity or reality. It is only necessary to improve one corner of this very valuable triangle in Scientology in order to improve the remaining two corners. Also called the ARC triangle.

5. **castigate:** criticize or reprimand severely.

sanity. Even so, it will require of us and our children a special kind of discipline if we are to make up even a scintilla[6] of the lost time.

About discipline there are as many theories as there are feathers on a duck. Actually, however, they boil down to two considerations: what does or what does not act as compulsion against self-determinism? Do a little self-examination. When do you do your best work: when you are compelled, or when you are led into making your own decisions by understanding reasons behind what needs to be done?

The ARC triangle again plays a big part. You maintain communication only when you have understanding. Understanding builds reality. You feel affinity only for that which is real for you. One will imposed on another is compulsion. Compulsion immediately knocks out communication. How do you feel when husband, wife or boss arbitrarily says "You do it my way or else"? Your child feels the same way. Compulsion is an arbitrary. It may block communication, blunt affinity and deny reality. If any one of these aspects of the triangle is mitigated[7] or vitiated,[8] the other two aspects are automatically affected adversely, too. On the other hand, don't you feel good when someone says to you, "Your idea has a lot of merit; how will it fit in here? How will it affect the situation? What will happen if we use your idea?"

Study the effects of compulsive discipline. Try to derive methods which will not aberrate the child, but increase his data and help him to form his own decisions. Here specific problems for home testing will assist toward attaining full understanding.

---

6. **scintilla:** a minute particle; spark; trace.

7. **mitigated:** lessened in force or severity.

8. **vitiated:** debased; corrupted; perverted.

Apparently the factor we as parents find most difficult to comprehend is "What is important?" If we can learn to ask ourselves the question "Is it important?" we will have solved perhaps seventy-five percent of our problems. This question posed immediately will often prevent the unreeling of a dramatization over something the child has done. An example is the spilled glass of milk. Is it important? Was it done on purpose? Which is more rational: *dramatizing* your restimulated anger, which may key in or restimulate a lock in the child, or cleaning up the mess with a smile while helping him to analyze the need for carefulness?

Control circuits have been mentioned. Control circuits are quite often activated by compulsive discipline. Such phrases as: "Control yourself," "You do what you're told," "You're nothing but a cry baby," "You must be a big man and not cry," only contribute to a child's irrational behavior. Unless you want to spend hours running out circuitry at a later date, you will find it profitable to avoid installing it.

You should seek to increase your child's self-determinism, his reliance on his analyzer, and help him to be independent of you and of his reactive mind.

There is a difference between self-determinism and selfish determination. A self-determined person is one who acts after analytical computation, taking into consideration all data available as to the effect of the proposed action on himself *and on other people!* Selfish determination is the aberrated evaluation of data as they affect only one's self.

Compulsion is much broader than just that phase of it which applies to discipline. An individual may be as much compelled from within as from without. Do not be afraid to air your problems and your aberrations in your group. If you are afraid of what the group will think of you, use the importance test. Remember that fear is also aberration. Is it more important to solve these problems and build a happy family, or is it more important to keep these other people from guessing that you have aberrations? (As though they don't know!)

Education: What do you know about your schools? Your children spend a good portion of their lives there. The group may devote part of its time profitably to discovering how and what the children are taught. You will discover that in most schools the work is designed for "normal" children. The exceptionally bright or the especially slow are not usually handled with any individuality.

Consider degrees of alertness or intelligence. As your own processing continues your computational ability will increase and your energy level will rise. The improvement in your recalls will astonish you. Does this tell you anything about the difference in children? Is the child slow for reasons not hitherto understood? His recalls may be occluded, making it difficult for him to remember anything. Or he may have engrams (and where did he get them?) that tell him he is no good, has no initiative, will never amount to anything, etc. Result: a slow child.

On the other hand, take the "bright" child. He may be bright because he relies on memory, having no engrams to prevent his recalls. In this case he can remember everything he has perceived. The early years of school will be simple for him, as most of the work is based on memory and is unoccluded. Later, however, when he gets into such abstract[9] subjects as higher

---

9. **abstract:** concerned with ideas or concepts rather than actual particulars or instances; not practical or applied; ideal or theoretical.

mathematics and the sciences, he may begin to slip if he continues to rely on memory. Memory is fine, but the individual who has learned to rely solely upon his memory may not have developed the ability for abstract reasoning.

The child with blocked perceptic recalls is slower because he is obliged to use reasoning processes to compute the answers to problems. Such children may flounder, especially in schools geared to so-called "normal" recalls. There is no time for the slow child.

What can you do to help the slow child sharpen his perceptics, keep them sharp and develop recall? What can you do to help the child with unusually sharp perceptics and good recall, to develop his reasoning processes?

In solving these problems, straight line memory is an invaluable technique. Games will also aid the development of these processes. Discuss such things in your group.

Education is an extremely broad field. In a democracy the schools belong to you. Insist on sound methods of instruction, and your children will receive them. But what is sound instruction? Dianetics forces a complete reevaluation here, as in every other field of living. Groups of parents who discuss and formulate these things will determine the future of education.

Playground Workshop: Your child is an individual. He is also part of society. He must learn to get along happily with others. How does your youngster do in this respect?

As a part of the group's activity there may be planned programs of play, stories and handicraft. These could take place once or twice each month on Saturdays when more children are free. Parents might take turns in leading the activities for groups of various ages while other parents observe. It would be best if each parent present observed someone else's child at least fifty percent of the time. The results of these observations could then be discussed and new teaching methods developed to help correct errors in handling the children. A parent will gain a better insight into her child's makeup when observing him at play with other children.

Conclusion

Quite a lot of questions here, aren't there?

The answers are here in this book and there in your lives.

In addition to straight processing, you will find Dianetic ideas extremely useful in the home. With a sound knowledge of such things as the significance of the ARC triangle, you will soon realize that when you invalidate anything your child, husband or wife says, you are reducing that person's sense of reality, breaking affinity and blocking communication. When you doubt something another says, ask yourself, "Is it important?" If it is important for the item to be corrected, use questions to bring out the correct information. And remember, *you* may be the one who is wrong.

Another ARC break results from withholding information. When you refrain from telling another something he wants to know you will find affinity weakened.

Even if families do not engage in active processing, the observation of a few Dianetic "do's" can have amazing results in raising the family tone. Check yourself and your family on these:

1. Do everything possible to maintain affinity, reality and communication.

2. Use discipline based on understanding and computation rather than on compulsion.

3. Use the question, "Is it important?" before taking any precipitate[10] action.

4. Realize that *any* invalidation of another's data adversely affects the ARC triangle.

5. Pass on information the other person should have instead of concealing the facts in the hope of saving the other some anguish, but do not burden the child with adult problems.

6. Remember, the family is a team and an ARC break with one member is a break with all.

7. Watch for possible key-in and restimulating phrases and actions, and avoid them until they can be erased.

8. Watch for control circuit phrases and avoid them.

This could well be considered a Dianetic family code. As your group works on the problems suggested, you will see the wisdom of following the points listed above. In fact, you will probably be able to add to and clarify the items as you go along.

Specific Suggestions: Since it is best, due to similarity of reactive banks, for parents not to process their own children, if it can be avoided, it is suggested that parents form teams, when possible, with other parents to exchange auditing for their children. Children *in general* are best audited by members of their own sex. And quite frequently young auditors will do better

10. **precipitate:** done or made without sufficient deliberation; overhasty; rash.

than other Dianeticists in auditing children, as younger persons are still close to the problems, perplexities and disappointments of childhood. However, an older auditor with a natural aptitude and a true understanding of children should never be disqualified because of his age.

Since Dianetic processing takes time, children may resent it. They may feel that their time is better spent in play, in enjoying friendships, in accumulating all the enriching experience suitable to their age. If a child is happy in his environment, well adjusted to those around him, pursuing a successful child's life, perhaps it is best to leave well enough alone and do no Dianetic processing beyond a little straight line memory work occasionally to blow locks, and the running of pleasure moments to relieve the tedium of long train or auto trips. Children are jealous of their time, and we as adults should recognize this and respect it.

But when a child shows unhappiness, or suffers from chronic somatics such as asthma, hay fever and other allergies, or has any other indication of suboptimum function, then there is a place for Dianetic processing. Pleasure moments and straight line memory can be used again and again. As you grow increasingly skillful in the use of straight line memory, you may key out the chronic somatic, or the source of mental upset. Use pleasure moments to bring up the child's sense of affinity, reality and communication. After he has been "run" a few times in pleasure, the child will begin to look forward to his processing and will not begrudge the time devoted to it.

Care should be used never to allow Dianetic processing to usurp the place of "more important" affairs such as watching the football game on television, or going to a party, or anything else the child values. This would place Dianetics among the nonsurvival factors in his life and make him resent it.

When a parent has to process his own child, he should first

be audited himself, progressing as far along the road as time allows before he undertakes the child's processing. Not only is the child subject to restimulation by the parent, but the parent may be restimulated by the child. Too often the child's dramatization furnishes the "other side" of the parent's dramatization. And of course, generally speaking, fully half the material in the child's engram bank is derived from the parent and is likely to be discovered in the parent's bank, also. Therefore, the parent should have his own engrams at least well deintensified, and his own temperament stabilized very thoroughly before he attempts to process his child. Otherwise, he may lose his impersonal approach and his temper, break the Auditor's Code, establish new locks on the child's old locks, and by breaking affinity as an auditor make affinity as a parent doubly difficult to reestablish.

For proper use of the material in this book it will be especially helpful to read and use the material in two other publications: *Dianetics: The Modern Science of Mental Health* and *Self Analysis* by L. Ron Hubbard. Dianetic processing must be understood and preferably should have been practiced on at least several adults before the auditor attempts to process a child.

12

Child Guidance Centers

12

Child Guidance Centers

The following material is intended to serve as an outline in setting up Child Guidance Centers. None of the material is presented as definitive. These are suggestions only, but they are based on practical application and experience at a Child Guidance Center in Southern California which had been operating for several months when this material was compiled; they have been found to be sound where used.

Child Guidance Centers may be established by Dianetic groups, by professional auditors or by parents in cooperation with each other. Centers, whenever possible, should be run by lay[1] personnel who devote themselves to the smooth functioning of the Center, attending to all necessary details. Centers should employ one or more (preferably two) trained auditors specializing in child guidance. Professional auditors so employed should be free to devote all working time to the children.

Some of the preliminary material contained in this chapter will concern only the lay personnel; the rest is the concern of professional auditors who have chosen or will choose Child Dianetics as their speciality.

---

1. **lay:** not belonging to, connected with or proceeding from a profession.

Physical surroundings, like those of any good nursery school, should be cheerful and informal. There should be a room large enough to play in, containing a table for finger-painting activities close to a low sink for washing hands. There should be a smaller room for parent interviews.

The Center should own the following equipment:

Small toys: at least three sets of mama and papa dolls, baby dolls, small boy and girl dolls, larger boy and girl dolls; dolls of policemen, firemen, nurses, doctors; wild animal toys (lions, tigers, wildcats, boars, snakes); peaceful animal toys (horses, kittens, cats, dogs, elephants, bears); sticks, fences, shrubbery, garages, houses, schools, hospitals.

Play materials appropriate for the age group: clay, Plasticine,[2] buttons, water paints, punching bags, telephones, rubber suction darts, bridges, stoves and cooking utensils, motor toys, crayons, blackboard and chalk, tools and leather, shell work, wood-burning instruments, dominoes, storybooks.

Toys should be simple and should stimulate the children's fantasy. Do not bar ugly toys, nor try to keep the toys in perfect condition. Children like old toys. Observe the use the children make of the toys and what they say about them.

Stock a supply of nursing bottles and nipples and simple sterilizing equipment; also bathroom furniture, as frequently the first key-ins occur during toilet training.

For finger painting: procure any starch free of foreign particles; boil a quart of it very thick, add one teaspoon salt, one-half

2. **Plasticine:** a brand name for a synthetic material used as a substitute for clay or wax in modeling.

cup of soap flakes while hot, two ounces of glycerine;[3] stir well. Finger painting tempera:[4] blue, red, yellow, white, brown and black. Mix your own colors in plastic cereal dishes: two teaspoons of tempera to about six ounces of starch. Mix while warm. Paint on the glazed side of finger-paint paper or glossy shelf paper, after dipping in water. The paints will work easily if the glazed side is slightly damp.

Make a comprehensive inventory[5] of each child. Child processing also takes into consideration the home and general environment of the child. When the parents come in to relate the child's problems, a fairly verbatim account of what the mother says should be taken down. Frequently the auditor is able to locate the constant restimulation in this first interview with the mother.

It is suggested that the following questions be asked, as well as such other questions as further experience may indicate to be valuable:

Name and reasons for choosing the child's first name, age, sex, religion. Does the child attend Sunday school? Mother's occupation and hobbies. Father's occupation and hobbies. If both parents work, who cares for the child?

Ailments of Mother. Ailments of Father. (Frequently illnesses of the parents will indicate sympathy engrams passed on

---

3. **glycerin:** same as *glycerol*, a colorless, sweet, syrupy liquid obtained from animal and vegetable oils and fats. Glycerol is used as a solvent, in lotions and ointments, in explosives, and in antifreezes.

4. **tempera:** a painting medium in which pigment is mixed with water-soluble glutinous materials.

5. **inventory:** the gathering of data for the auditor's use in resolving the case, during which he establishes affinity with the preclear.

from parents to children by contagion of aberration, as well as chronic bouncers: "Get away from Daddy now. He doesn't feel good.")

Conditions during the child's prenatal life. Did the mother have morning sickness? Falls, accidents, other ailments? Were there attempted abortions or contraceptive douches after becoming pregnant before the mother knew of the fact? Hours in labor? Was birth easy or difficult? Was anesthesia used? Was the cord around the neck? Was there any difficulty in getting the child to breathe?

What was the child's first illness? Did he ever fall off the bed? Are there older children? Were any of the other children ill or did they suffer any accidents before the child was born? Any illnesses or accidents since? Have there been any operations on the child? List them. Has the child been to a doctor lately? Doctor's summary of present state of health. Was the sex of the baby satisfactory to both parents? Were there other persons living in the home before the baby was born? What were their attitudes toward the mother having this baby?

Check for indications of chronic somatics:

Feeding and digestion (if disturbed, usually indicate a rejected child): food rejections, vomiting, allergies.

Breathing: Hay fever, asthma, bronchitis.

Elimination: Bed-wetting and soiling.

Sex: Excessive masturbation, other sex acts, cruelties.

Nervous habits: Thumb sucking, nail biting.

Overactivity: Restlessness.

Lethargy: Low physical activity.

Hysterical spells: Dizziness, fainting, convulsions, temper tantrums.

Chronic dramatizations.

Emotions: Anxieties and fears, petulance, unhappiness.

Social reactions: Shyness, aggressiveness, resentments, disobedience, jealousy.

Speech: Retarded speech, faulty enunciation, baby talk, lisping and stuttering.

Mental functions: Thought blocking, memory lapses, fantasies, daydreaming.

Compensations: Symbolic actions, obsessions, exaggerated needs, greeds.

Play: Destructive, lack of energy, complete boredom.

Work: Lack of concentration, lack of interest, laziness, difficulty in learning problems.

Moral values: Lack of responsibility, lack of self-criticism, over self-criticism, hyperconsciousness, perfectionism, atoning, wrong independence, lying, cheating, stealing.

Whom does the child resemble? Is he "just like" someone else in the home?

Does the child seem attentive when spoken to or is he a victim of "You never listen to a thing I say!"?

Does the child have visual difficulties ("I can't see . . . "
etc.)?

The auditor should develop a system of general procedure,
for which the following practices have been found workable.

In the first interview with the parents, the auditor tries to
discover the child's chief engrams and the consistent dramatizations of the parents which may have been keyed in for the child.

The inventory and preliminary interview with the parents
establishes communication by a permissive attitude and sympathetic listening. Affinity may be increased by a short explanation
of the contagion of aberration, from parent through children to
the children's children. Dianetics, now that the removal of aberration is possible, overcomes any guilt for the planting of aberrations, and allows parents to help their children and themselves.

After the first interview with the parents the child should be
brought and left for at least three sessions with the professional
auditor. Often it will be discovered that the child's real problem is
none of the things the parents have been so ready to discuss, but
something else that the parents have ignored or have not observed.

Does the mother seem overprotective? Look for sympathy
engrams in the child or possibly antagonism from the father (or
both). The same is true in reverse.

In the first session with the child, the primary objective is to
establish affinity through communication. Without being told so,
the child should be made to feel that there is no blame of any
kind for anything that may have been done or will be said.
Children need a sympathetic listener. Help them to know that
you can see from their viewpoint. Be completely permissive with

them. Never give negative instructions; use positive suggestions.

Children may further communicate through color (finger painting). Children will often unknowingly put their emotions on paper. Let them play in the paints. The paint in the plastic cereal bowls will avoid the fear and trials of breakage. Have the painting table close to the sink, and let the children dip into the water when they wish to do so.

Observe what colors are chosen and what the children talk about as they use the colors. Observe the mass (where it is placed), form, spaces and emotional reaction to the colors being used. Children paint what they feel.

Deep sighs while using the color of brown frequently indicate difficulties in connection with toilet training, grief and a possible holder: "You bad boy! Sit right there on the potty; I'll teach you to mess your panties!" It frequently takes very adroit questioning to lead the child into running these incidents. Do not be discouraged if during the first three sessions the child does not return to any specific incident.

Establishing affinity and communication is the most important objective. Work to raise the tone level of the child and to get him up to present time. Strive to make the processing a pleasure incident for the child, through your understanding of his difficulties and the permissive atmosphere. You will frequently find that this is the first time in his life that he has been allowed to play or express himself without constant direction. At first, if this is the case, you may have to help him a little in his play. However, you will soon find that he has few difficulties in your presence as soon as he recognizes that you are not going to punish or scold.

Have him make a toy set-up for you of school, home,

Grandma's and other places he frequents. Where does he place himself in these surroundings? Does he seem to be alone, separate from the rest? If so, ask, "Who says, 'I'm all alone, the world?' or 'You're all on your own now.' " Ask him to tell you about the time he heard Grandma (or whoever it was) say, "I'm all alone in the world" or "Nobody loves me." Children usually like to tell about the dramatic things that happen in their world, and will usually give you a vivid picture of Papa and Mama dramatizing.

Does the child choose only the wild animals to play with? One little girl had nightmares of a lion who was going to eat her and her mother. In returning to the incident that was causing the nightmares, Father was found screaming at Mother, "You're a-lyin' to me!" In the child's lack of understanding, "lyin' " automatically became the lion seen in the zoo.

One little girl who had a great deal of difficulty in school was found to be living with a grandmother whose constant phrase was, "Don't tell anybody anything about—(almost any subject from Mother to cookie cutters). It's none of their business."

The first three interviews should serve to determine the child's troubles. Through selection of toys which the child makes, the auditor can frequently determine just where the child is stuck on the time track.

Does an eight-year-old choose a nursing bottle and spend most of her time filling it with water and "playing baby"? Look for the key-in that took place during the time she was a nursing baby, possibly Mother saying, "Hold still, now."

As soon as possible get the child to talk. He will usually speak of the things that are bothering him. Play "remembering" games with the children, and in this way have them run the affinity, reality, communication locks. Possibly one of the best times for this is while they are finger painting.

One of the most valuable aids for children is to educate them by treating as locks any information they have picked up which is confusing to them. Is there confusion in the child's mind about death, birth, marriage or any of the other common subjects which adults discuss without bothering to explain to the child? If anything is worrying him, he will usually either tell about it directly or picture it in his play.

After the first three sessions with the child, both parents should come in for an interview, together, if possible, and have a frank discussion of some of the child's difficulties. The child must never be present on such occasions, lest he be restimulated and the parents hampered in their discussion of personal or intimate matters.

In this interview much tact will have to be exercised. Neither parent should be alienated,[6] but there will be factors needing correction in the home. Usually the parents will be willing to cooperate in dropping the use of phrases that are too restimulative to the child. Frequently they will be anxious for processing on themselves in order to overcome their dramatizations. It should be made clear to the parents at this time that it may take a great deal of work, both on the auditor's part and theirs, to give the child a Release. In some cases it is possible to release a child within a very few sessions; in many others it may take months. Therefore, evaluation of time necessary to release the child should not be made. This is especially important when processing children whose parents have brought them in for specific reasons.

6. **alienated:** made indifferent or hostile.

In Child Dianetics it is necessary that the auditor have a natural affinity for children, plus an ability to meet the children on their own level. Auditors who become impatient with children cannot expect to accomplish efficient processing.

In addition to interviews and professional processing, it is wise to organize group play activity for several children under the supervision and observation of trained observers.

Observers should record the activity and conversation of the children playing in a group. Later the auditor will evaluate the observations and make recommendations to the parents or others who care for the children. Observation of this sort is not as valuable nor as exact as that obtained during the Dianetic processing of a child, but it may be utilized very effectively where there seems to be no extreme or pressing aberration.

For the guidance center which attempts group activities, larger toys will be needed, such as swings, merry-go-rounds, sandboxes, shovels, pails and games which increase cooperation. There will be more direction of the children in play, and a definite effort to increase any special skills or talents which the children may exhibit.

From these groups it is often possible to select the child or children most in need of processing. Any child who is a consistent misfit in the group will be found to be suffering from restimulated engrams and should have private processing.

In general, in any community where there is a desire among its citizens, child guidance centers may be set up by volunteer gifts of time and property. This limits current expenses to the employment of auditors and specialists in the supervision of children.

Wherever possible, a larger budget will allow a more efficient and businesslike maintenance of services to the community and its children.

13

Summary

13

Summary

A. Preventive Dianetics

1. Observe silence during and for several minutes after moments of pain and anaten at all ages. Especially important are:

Prenatal life:

Be silent during and after the sex act.

During pregnancy be silent at times of injury, during applications of first aid, doctor's examinations, illness and operations involving the expectant mother.

Be silent but helpful after electric shocks, bumps and jars to the mother's body.

Be silent after the mother coughs or sneezes.

Arrange for silence when a general anesthesia is administered to the mother. Where there is a choice, local anesthesia is always preferable.

If your aberrations, environment or social set compel you to drink to excess, for posterity's sake learn to do it in complete silence.

Birth:

Arrange for absolute silence during labor and birth.

2. Observe silence during moments of emotional disturbances involving the expectant mother or child. During moments of crying or fear, rub the preclear's back firmly and gently, preferably with skin contact, but *be silent* and make all physical movements slow and understandable. Do not argue with, or within the hearing of mother or child.

3. Prevent restimulation at all ages by noting dramatizations and their restimulators. Refrain from using restimulators; restate them in other words, change a restimulative environment. Prevent sympathy computations.

4. At all times express affinity for the child, allow him his own sense of reality and permit him to communicate.

5. Discipline the child in silence. Explain to him your reasons for discipline, prior to or subsequent to pain and anaten.

B. Educational Dianetics

1. Supply relatively correct data to the analyzer at all times.

2. Supply information about Dianetics to all concerned. It is especially important to educate doctors, nurses and mothers to the desperate need for silent and natural childbirth and the need for silent care in handling the newborn baby.

3. Establish goals for the child, especially that of adulthood.

4. Establish a definite program of acquiring bodily skills, using guidance without force.

C. Dianetic First Aid

1. In addition to proper medical care, run the child in revrie, if possible, immediately after moments of pain and anaten, as soon as the analyzer is functioning again. With smaller children, in place of reverie, use straight line memory technique: "What happened?"And go over it until the child is bored or amused.

2. In addition to medical first aid, teach the child to run out minor cuts, burns and scratches immediately after receiving them. (Close the eyes and return to the moment of injury, and run it several times with as many perceptics as possible.)

3. Keep records of engramic moments, emotional disturbances during prenatal life and prior to the availability of the child for processing; also records of members of the household and their dramatizations. Be as exact as possible. These records should be made available to the child's auditor when the child is ready for processing.

D. Dianetic Processing

1. From the time the child begins to speak, use straight line memory technique on locks, controls and valence shifts.

2. Do not invalidate the child's sense of reality; honor the Auditor's Code.

3. Reorient the child semantically, by treating reception of original faulty information as a lock.

4. From the age of eight, run the child in reverie: pleasure, grief and locks.

5. From the age of twelve, process the child, using Standard Procedure as outlined in *Science of Survival.*

6. Restate any Dianetic term if it contains a charge for the child, or treat the receipt of the charge as a lock.

E. Things to Remember

1. Recognize that the authority on identifying as well as treating organic ills, germ-borne diseases, is your physician. If possible, choose one who is a Dianeticist or knows his Dianetics.

2. Be familiar with methods of medical first aid.

3. Observe the precepts of preventive medicine and efficient nutrition.

Appendix

Appendix A

The Auditor's Code

The auditor conducts himself in such a way as to maintain optimum affinity, communication and agreement with the preclear.

The auditor is trustworthy. He understands that the preclear has given into the auditor's trust his hope for higher sanity and happiness, and that trust is sacred and never to be betrayed.

The auditor is courteous. He respects the preclear as a human being. He respects the self-determinism of the preclear. He respects his own position as an auditor. He expresses this respect in courteous conduct.

The auditor is courageous. He never falls back from his duty to a case. He never fails to use the optimum procedure regardless of any alarming conduct on the part of the preclear.

The auditor never evaluates the case for the preclear. He abstains from this, knowing that to compute for the preclear is to inhibit the preclear's own computation. He knows that to refresh the preclear's mind as to what went before is to cause the preclear to depend heavily upon the auditor and so to undermine the self-determinism of the preclear.

The auditor never invalidates any of the data or the personality of the preclear. He knows that in doing so he would seriously enturbulate the preclear. He refrains from criticism and invalidation, no matter how much the auditor's own sense of reality is twisted or shaken by the preclear's incidents or utterances.

The auditor uses only techniques designed to restore the self-determinism of the preclear. He refrains from all authoritarian or dominating conduct, leading always rather than driving. He refrains from the use of hypnotism or sedatives on the preclear no matter how much the preclear may demand them out of aberration. He never abandons the preclear out of faintheartedness about the ability of techniques to resolve the case, but persists and continues to restore the preclear's self-determinism. The auditor keeps himself informed of any new skills in the science.

The auditor cares for himself as an auditor. By working with others he maintains his own processing at regular intervals in order to maintain or raise his own position on the Tone Scale despite restimulation of himself through the process of auditing others. He knows that failure to give heed to his own processing, until he himself is a Release or a Clear in the severest meaning of the terms, is to cost his preclear the benefit of the auditor's best performance.

Dianetics and Language

One can consider that the missions of the energy of life, or at least one of them, is the creation, conservation, maintenance, acquisition, destruction, change, occupation, grouping and dispersal of matter, energy, space and time, which are the component factors of the material universe.

So long as an individual maintains his own belief in his ability to handle the physical universe and organisms about him and to control them if necessary or to work in harmony with them, and to make himself competent over and among the physical universe of his environment, he remains healthy, stable and balanced and cheerful. It is only after he discovers his inabilities in handling organisms, matter, energy, space and time, and when these things have been sharply painful to him, that he begins to decline physically, become less competent mentally, and to fail in life. These questions are aimed toward the rehabilitation of his ability to handle organisms and the physical universe.

It was a pre-Dianetic error that an individual was healthy so long as he was adjusted to his environment. Nothing could be less workable than this "adaptive" postulate and had anyone cared to compare it with actuality he would have discovered that the success of man depends upon his ability to master and change his environment. Man succeeds because he adjusts his environment to *him,* not by adjusting himself to the environment. The "adjusted" postulate is indeed a viciously dangerous one, since it seeks to indoctrinate the individual into the belief that he must be a slave to his environment. The philosophy is dangerous because the people so indoctrinated can be enslaved in that last of all graveyards, a welfare state. However, this postulate is very handy in case one wishes to subjugate or nullify human beings for his own ends. The effort in the direction of adjusting men to their environment by giving them "social training," by punishing them if they are bad, and by otherwise attempting to subdue and break them, has filled the society's prisons and insane asylums to the bursting point. Had anyone cared to look at the real universe he would have found this to be true: No living organism can be broken by force into an adjusted state and still remain able and amiable. Any horse trainer, for instance, knows that the horse must not be pushed or broken into submission if one wishes to retain his abilities, but, as they used to say in the army, mules were far more expensive than men, and perhaps it was not in the interest of pre-Dianetic thought to preserve men in a happy state. However, one should not be too harsh on these previous schools of thought since they had no knowledge of the natural laws of thought and in the absence of these, criminals can only be punished and not cured and the insane can only be driven down into the last dregs of tractability. The nearer to death, according to those schools of thought, the better, as witness electric shock "therapy" and brain surgery—those efforts on the part of the mental medical men to as closely approximate euthanasia[1] as possible without crossing the border into the legal fact of death. These past schools have now been taken under the wing of Dianetics, which embraces all

---

1. **euthanasia:** the action of inducing a painless death of a person for reasons assumed to be merciful.

fields of thought, and are being reeducated. It is found that they quickly desert the punishment-drive "therapies" as soon as they completely understand that they are not necessary, now that the natural laws of thought and behavior are known. One cannot, however, wholly repress a shudder at the fate of the hundreds of thousands of human guinea pigs whose lives and persons were ruined by the euthanistic methods employed in the dark ages of unreason.

Your health depends almost entirely upon your confidence in your ability to handle the physical universe about you and to change and adjust your environment so that you can survive in it. It is actually an illusion that you cannot ably handle your environment, an illusion implanted by aberrated people in the past, during moments when you were unconscious and could not defend yourself or when you were small and were directed and misdirected and given pain and sorrow and upset, and had no way to effect your right to handle yourself in your environment.

On Lake Tanganyika[2] the natives have a very interesting way of catching fish. There on the equator the sun shines straight down through the clear water. The natives take blocks of wood and string them along a long rope. They stretch this rope between two canoes and with these abreast begin to paddle toward the shoal water. By the time they have reached the shoals, schools of fish are piled and crowded into the rocks and onto the beach. The blocks of wood on the rope made shadows which went all the way down to the bottom of the lake and the fish, seeing the approach of these shadows and the apparent solid bars which they formed in the water, swam fearfully away from them and so were caught.

---

2. **Lake Tanganyika:** lake in central Africa, between Zaire and Tanzannia. The longest freshwater lake in the world, about 450 miles long, 30–40 miles wide.

A man can be driven and harassed and worked upon by aberrated people about him until he too conceives shadows to be reality. Should he simply reach out toward them, he would discover how thin and penetrable they are. His usual course, however, is to retreat from them and at last find himself in the shadows of bad health, broken dreams and an utter disownment of himself and the physical universe.

A considerable mechanical background of the action and peculiarities of the energy of thought makes it possible for these lists to bring about the improved state of being that they do, when properly used; but over and above these mechanical aspects, the simple recognition that there have been times in one's life when he did control the physical universe as needful, when he was in harmony with organisms about him, validates the reality of his ability.

Caught up by the illusion of words, stressed into obedience when he was a child by physical means, man is subject to his greatest shadow and illusion—*language*. The words, forcefully spoken, "Come here!" have no actual physical ability to draw the individual to the speaker. Yet he may approach, although he may be afraid to do so. He is impelled in his approach because he has been made to "come here" by physical force so many times in the early period of his life, while the words "come here" were being spoken, that he is trained much like a dog to obey a signal. The physical force which made him approach is lost to view and in its place stands the shadow "come here"; thus, to that degree he loses his self-determinism on the subject of "come here." As life goes on, he makes the great error of supposing that any and all words have force and importance. With words, those about him plant their shadow cages. They restrict him from doing this; they compel him to do that—and almost hour by hour and day by day he is directed by streams of words which in the ordinary society are not meant to help him but only to restrain him because of the fear of others. This Niagara of language is effective only because it substitutes for periods when he was physically impelled against his wishes to accept things he did not want, to care for things for which he actually had no use or liking, to go where he did not wish to go, and to do what he did not want to do. Language is quite acceptable when understood as a *symbol* for the act and thing, but the word *ashtray* is no substitute for an ashtray. If you do not believe this, try to put your ashes on the air waves which have just carried the word *ashtray*. Called a *saucer* or an *elephant*, the object intended for ashes serves just as well.

By the trick of language, then, and a magical, wholly unsubstantial trick it is, men seek to order the lives of men for their own advantage, and men caged about by the shadows observe and believe to their own detriment.

All languages derive from observation of matter, energy, space and time and other organisms in the environment. There is no word which is not derived and which does not have the connotation of the physical universe and other organisms.

Thus, when you answer these questions by recalling incidents which they evoke, be very sure that you do not evoke language incidents but action incidents. You do *not* want the time when you were *told* to do something—you want the time when you performed the *action*. You do not have to connect the language to the action in any way, but you will find as you answer questions on any of these lists that the value of language begins to depreciate considerably and that language strangely enough will become much more useful to you.

Can you recall a time when:

1. You moved an object.

2. An object moved you.

3. You threw an organism up into the air.

4. You walked downstairs.

5. You acquired something you wanted.

6. You created something good.

7. You felt big in a certain space.

8. You were proud to move something heavy.

9. You handled energy well.

10. You built a fire.

11. You lost something you didn't want.

12. You forced something on somebody.

13. You promoted survival.

14. You pleasantly expended time.

15. You closed in space.

16. You were master of your own time.

17. You opened up a space.

18. You handled a machine well.

19. You stopped a machine.

20. You raised an object.

21. You lowered yourself.

22. You destroyed something you didn't want.

23. You changed something for the better.

24. An organism you did not like moved away from you.

25. You obtained something you wanted.

26. You maintained a person.

27. You brought somebody you liked close to you.

28. You left a space you didn't like.

29. You conquered energy.

30. You destroyed a bad organism.

31. You handled fluid well.

32. You brought a number of pleasant objects together.

33. You placed a number of objects into space.

34. You threw unwanted objects away.

35. You dispersed many objects.

36. You tore an unwanted object to pieces.

37. You filled a space.

38. You regulated another's time.

39. You held an object close that you wanted.

40. You improved an object.

41. You emptied a space you wanted.

42. You went a distance.

43. You let time go.

44. You did what you wanted to do yourself.

45. You won out over an organism.

46. You got out from under domination.

47. You realized you were living your own life.

48. You knew you didn't have to do it.

49. You escaped from a dangerous space.

50. You entered upon a pleasant time.

Appendix C

Assists to Remembering

Remember is derived, of course, directly from action in the physical universe. How would a deaf-mute teach a child to remember? It would be necessary for him to keep forcing objects or actions on the child when the child left them alone or omitted them. Although parents are not deaf-mutes, children do not understand languages at very early ages, and as a consequence learn to *remember* by having their attention first called toward actions and objects, spaces and time. It violates the self-determinism of the individual, and therefore his ability to handle himself, to have things forced upon him without his agreement. This could be said to account, in part, for some of the "poor memories" about which people brag or complain.

Because one learns language at the level of the physical universe and action within it, he could be said to do with his thoughts what he has been compelled to do with the matter, energy, space and time in his environment. Thus, if these have been forced upon him and he did not want them, after a while he will begin to reject the thoughts concerning these objects, but if these objects, spaces and times and actions are forced upon him consistently enough he will at length go into an apathy about them. He will not want them very much but he thinks he has to accept them. Later on, in school, his whole livelihood seems to depend on whether or not he can remember the "knowledge" which is forced upon him.

The physical universe level of remembering, then, is retaining matter, energy, space and time. To improve the memory, it is only necessary to rehabilitate the individual's choice of acceptance of the material universe.

In answering these questions, particular attention should be paid to the happier incidents. Inevitably many unhappy incidents will flick through, but where selection is possible, happy or analytical incidents should be stressed. This list does not pertain to asking you to remember times when you remembered. It pertains to acquiring things which you wanted to acquire.

Can you remember a time when:

1. You acquired something you wanted.

2. You threw away something you didn't want.

3. You abandoned something you knew you were supposed to have.

4. You did something else with the time which was otherwise appointed for you.

5. You went into a space you were not supposed to occupy.

6. You left the place you were supposed to be.

7. You were happy to have acquired something you couldn't afford.

8. You happily defied directions you had been given.

9. You were sent to one place and chose to go to another.

10. You chose your own clothing.

11. You wore something in spite of what people would think.

12. You got rid of something which bored you.

13. You were glad to have choice over one of two objects.

14. You didn't drink any more than you wanted to.

15. You successfully refused to eat.

16. You did what you pleased with yourself.

17. You did what you pleased with a smaller person.

18. You were right not to have accepted something.

19. You gave away a present you had received.

20. You destroyed an object somebody forced upon you.

21. You had something you wanted and maintained it well.

22. You maliciously scuffed your shoes.

23. You didn't read the book you had been given.

24. You refused to be owned.

25. You changed somebody's orders.

26. You slept where you pleased.

27. You refused to bathe.

28. You spoiled some clothing and were cheerful about it.

29. You got what you wanted.

30. You got back something you had lost.

31. You got the person you wanted.

32. You refused a partner.

33. You threw the blankets off the bed.

34. You had your own way.

35. You found you had been right in refusing it.

About the Author

About the Author

L. Ron Hubbard is one of the most acclaimed and widely read authors of all time, primarily because his works express a firsthand knowledge of the nature of man—knowledge gained not from standing on the sidelines but through lifelong experience with people from all walks of life.

As Ron said, "One doesn't learn about life by sitting in an ivory tower, thinking about it. One learns about life by being part of it." And that is how he lived.

He began his quest for knowledge on the nature of man at a very early age. When he was eight years old he was already well on his way to being a seasoned traveler, covering a quarter of a million miles by the age of nineteen. His adventures included voyages to China, Japan and other points in the Orient and South Pacific. During this time he became closely acquainted with twenty-one different races in areas all over the world.

After returning to the United States, Ron pursued his formal studies of mathematics and engineering at George Washington University, where he was also a member of one of the first classes on nuclear physics. He realized that neither the East nor the West contained the full answer to the problems of existence.

Despite all of mankind's advances in the physical sciences, a *workable* technology of the mind and life had never been developed. The mental "technologies" which did exist, psychology and psychiatry, were actually barbaric, false subjects—no more workable than the methods of jungle witch doctors. Ron shouldered the responsibility of filling this gap in the knowledge of mankind.

He financed his early research through fiction writing. He became one of the most highly demanded authors in the golden age of popular adventure and science fiction writing during the 1930s and 1940s, interrupted only by his service in the U.S. Navy during World War II.

Partially disabled at the war's end, Ron applied what he had learned from his researches. He made breakthroughs and developed techniques which made it possible for him to recover from his injuries and help others to regain their health. It was during this time that the basic tenets of Dianetics technology were codified.

A year later, in 1948, he wrote the first manuscript detailing his discoveries. Ron did not have it published at that time, but gave copies to some friends who copied it and passed it among their friends who then passed it on to others. (This book was formally published in 1951 as *Dianetics: The Original Thesis* and later republished as *The Dynamics of Life*.) The interest generated by this manuscript prompted a flood of requests for more information on the subject.

Ron attempted to make all his discoveries available to the American Psychiatric Association and the American Medical Association. Despite the fact that his work would have benefited them and thereby society immensely, his offers were refused. These same vested interests decided that Dianetics could harm their profits (which were and still are based on the amount of illness and insanity in our culture) and began to attack Ron and his work. He therefore decided to write a comprehensive text on the subject and take it directly to the public.

With the publication of *Dianetics: The Modern Science of Mental Health* on May 9, 1950, a complete handbook for the application of Ron's new technology was broadly available for the first time. *Dianetics* created a wildfire of public interest. The book immediately shot to the top of the New York Times bestseller list and stayed there week after week. More than 750 Dianetics study groups sprang up within a few short months of its publication.

Ron kept on researching, improving methods and developing ways to advance other people's ability to apply Dianetics technology.

One of the areas Ron studied was the application of Dianetics to children. As Ron wrote, "When children become unimportant to a society, that society has forfeited its future." Accordingly, Ron developed special applications of his Dianetics discoveries for children not yet old enough to be aided with the main body of technology. Parents suddenly had methods of applying Dianetics to their offspring, nullifying with ease what others considered the unsolvable problems of childhood. People applying these techniques found they could build close, personal relationships with their children and create safe environments for their growth and development.

Ron's work did not stop with the successes of Dianetics. Further research led him to the basic truths of life itself and from these discoveries he developed Scientology, the first totally workable technology for the improvement of life.

The number of books and lectures continued to grow for

more than three decades as Ron kept on with his research into the mind and life.

Today Ron's works—including an astounding number of books, taped lectures, instructional films, writings, demonstrations and briefings—are studied and applied daily. Dianetics and Scientology techniques are used in hundreds of Hubbard Dianetics Foundations and Scientology organizations on every continent.

With his research fully completed and codified, L. Ron Hubbard departed his body on January 24, 1986.

Ron's work opened a new door for mankind. Through his efforts, there now exists a totally workable technology with which people can help each other improve their lives and succeed in achieving their goals.

Millions of people all over the world consider they have no truer friend.

Glossary

Aberrations: departures from rational thought or behavior. From the Latin, *aberrare*, to wander from; Latin, *ab*, away, *errare*, to wander. It means basically to err, to make mistakes, or more specifically to have fixed ideas which are not true. Aberration is opposed to sanity, which would be its opposite.

abstract: concerned with ideas or concepts rather than actual particulars or instances; not practical or applied; ideal or theoretical.

accessibility: the state of being willing to be processed (technical sense). The state of being willing to have interpersonal relations (social sense). For the individual himself, accessibility with self means whether or not an individual can recontact his past experiences or data. A man with a "bad memory" (interposed blocks between control center and facsimiles) has memories which are not accessible to him.

acidosis: a harmful condition in which the blood and tissues are less alkaline than is normal.

advent: coming or arrival.

affinity, reality and communication triangle: a triangle which is a symbol of the fact that affinity, reality and communication act together as a whole entity and that one of them cannot be considered unless the other two are also taken into account. Without affinity there is no reality or communication. Without reality or some agreement, affinity and communication are absent. Without communication there can be no affinity or reality. It is only necessary to improve one corner of this very valuable triangle in Scientology in order to improve the remaining two corners. Also called the ARC Triangle.

affinity: degree of liking or affection or lack of it. Affinity is a tolerance of distance. A great affinity would be a tolerance of or liking of close proximity. A lack of affinity would be an intolerance of or dislike of close proximity. Affinity is one of the components of understanding.

alienated: made indifferent or hostile.

allays: puts (fear, doubt, suspicion, anger, etc.) to rest; calms; quiets.

ally computations: little more than mere idiot calculations that anyone who is a friend can be kept a friend only by approximating the conditions wherein the friendship was realized. They are *computations* on the basis that one can only be safe in the vicinity of certain people and that one can only be in the vicinity of certain people by being sick or crazy or poor and generally disabled.

analytical mind: the conscious, aware mind which thinks, observes data, remembers it and resolves problems. It would be essentially the conscious mind as opposed to the unconscious mind. In Dianetics and Scientology the analytical mind is the one which is alert and aware and the reactive mind simply reacts without analysis.

assist: a simple, easily done process that can be applied to anyone to help them recover more rapidly from accidents, mild illness or upsets; any process which assists the individual to heal himself or be healed by another agency by removing his reasons for precipitating (bringing on) and prolonging his condition and lessening his predisposition (inclination or tendency) to further injure himself or remain in an intolerable condition.

asthma: a chronic disease that makes breathing difficult and causes coughing. Asthma is an allergy characterized by intermittent or continuous difficulty in breathing and a sense of constriction in the chest.

attenuated: weakened or reduced in force, intensity, effect, quantity or value.

auditor: a person trained and qualified in applying Dianetics and/or Scientology processes and procedures to individuals for their betterment; called an auditor because *auditor* means *one who listens.*

bank: *see* **reactive mind** in this glossary.

basic personality: the individual himself. The basic individual is not a buried unknown or a different person, but an intensity of all that is best and most able in the person.

basic-basic: the first moment of pain, anaten or discomfort in the current life of the individual.

beaverboard: a light, stiff sheeting made of wood fiber and used in building, especially for partitions or temporary structures.

brindle: having a gray or tawny coat streaked or spotted with a darker color.

castigate: criticize or reprimand severely.

Cesarean section: an operation by which a fetus is taken from the uterus by cutting through the walls of the abdomen and uterus.

chain: a succession of incidents, occurring at various intervals along the time track, that are related to one another by some similarity of either subject, general location, people or perception. Such a succession of similar incidents may span a brief period or a very long period of time.

charge: harmful energy or force accumulated and stored within the reactive mind, resulting from the conflicts and unpleasant experiences that a person has had. Auditing discharges this charge so that it is no longer there to affect the individual.

checks: restrains; holds in restraint or control.

chloroform: a colorless liquid with a sharp, sweetish smell and taste. Chloroform evaporates quickly and easily. When its vapor is inhaled, it makes a person unconscious or unable to feel pain.

complex: *psychology,* an idea or group of repressed ideas associated with a past emotional disturbance so as to influence a person's present behavior to a great or excessive degree.

comport: bear or conduct (themselves); behave.

credence: belief as to the truth of something.

cyst: a small sac in animals or plants, usually containing liquid and diseased matter produced by inflammation. Cysts are often caused by the blocking of some passage, for example in a gland.

demons: mechanical mechanisms set up by an engram which take over a portion of the analyzer and act as individual beings A bonafide demon is one who gives thoughts voice or echoes the spoken word interiorly or who gives all sorts of complicated advice like a real, live voice exteriorly.

dramatizations: duplications of engramic content, entire or in part, by an aberree (aberrated person) in his present-time environment. Aberrated conduct is entirely dramatization. When dramatizing, the individual is like an actor playing his dictated part and going through a whole series of irrational actions.

dub-in: unknowingly created mental pictures that appear to have been a record of the physical universe but are, in fact, only altered copies of the time track. It is a phrase out of the motion-picture industry of putting a sound track on top of something that isn't there.

dwindling spiral: a phenomenon of the ARC triangle whereby when one breaks some affinity, a little bit of the reality goes down, and then communication goes down, which makes it impossible to get affinity as high as before; so a little bit more gets knocked off affinity, and then reality goes down, and then communication. This is the dwindling spiral in progress, until it hits the bottom—death—which is no affinity, no communication and no reality.

efficacy: capacity for producing a desired result or effect; effectiveness.

encephalitis: inflammation of the brain caused by injury, infection, poison or other agent. Sleeping sickness is one kind of encephalitis.

engram: a mental image picture which is a recording of an experience containing pain, unconsciousness and a real or fancied threat to survival. It is a recording in the reactive mind of something which actually happened to an individual in the past and which contained pain and unconsciousness, both of which are recorded in the mental image picture called an engram. It must, by definition, have impact or injury as part of its content. These engrams are a complete recording, down to the last accurate detail, of every perception present in a moment of partial or full unconsciousness.

environ: abbreviation for environment.

esteem: hold to be; consider; regard.

euthanasia: the action of inducing a painless death of a person for reasons assumed to be merciful.

ex-barbers: those who were once barbers. This is a satirical reference to the fact that modern physicians, and therefore the American Medical Association, are descended from barbers. The barber was the original surgeon, performing mainly the pulling of teeth and bloodletting (in addition to the usual cutting of beards and hair). The surgeon separated out as a profession directly from the barber's craft, and then the surgeon became a physician.

flash-answer: of or characteristic of a first flash response. The *flash answer* is an instantaneous reply, the first thing that flashes into the preclear's mind at the snap of the auditor's fingers.

Foundation: the Hubbard Dianetic Research Foundation, the first organization of Dianetics. It was first located in Elizabeth, New Jersey and later in Wichita, Kansas.

Freud: Sigmund Freud (1856–1939), Austrian neurologist, founder of psychoanalysis.

gastritis: inflammation of the stomach, especially of its mucous membrane.

Genghis Khan: (1162–1227) Mongol conqueror of most of Asia and of east Europe to the Dnieper River.

geometric progression: a sequence of terms in which the ratio between any two successive terms is the same, as the progression 1, 3, 9, 27, 81 or 144, 12, 1, $\frac{1}{12}$, $\frac{1}{144}$.

glycerin: same as *glycerol*, a colorless, sweet, syrupy liquid obtained from animal and vegetable oils and fats. Glycerol is used as a solvent, in lotions and ointments, in explosives, and in antifreezes.

goblins: grotesque sprites or elves that are mischievous or malicious toward people.

HDA: an abbreviation for Hubbard Dianetics Auditor, a person who has been trained to deliver auditing as described in *Dianetics: The Modern Science of Mental Health.*

hellion: a disorderly, troublesome, rowdy or mischievous person.

hookah: a tobacco pipe of Near Eastern origin with a long, flexible tube by which the smoke is drawn through a jar of water and thus cooled.

Hopalong Cassidy: a cowboy hero in a series of western movies made in the 1930s.

humane society: a group of persons organized to protect children or animals from cruelty.

implicit: potential contained (in).

indomitable: not easily discouraged, defeated or subdued; unyielding; unconquerable.

insidious: operating or proceeding in an inconspicuous or seemingly harmless way but actually with grave effect.

insurgent: a person who rises in revolt; rebel.

inventory: the gathering of data for the auditor's use in resolving the case, during which he establishes affinity with the preclear.

Irish mail: a toy handcar.

jags: a period of unrestrained indulgence in an activity; spree; binge.

Jeans, Sir James: (1877–1946) English astrophysicist and author.

Jesuits: members of a Roman Catholic religious order (Society of Jesus) founded by Ignatius of Loyola in 1534. Mainly a missionary order, the Jesuits used education as its primary means of propagating their beliefs.

Junior cases: cases which have the characteristic of sharing the same name as a parent. Let's say the father's name was George and the patient's name was George, the engram bank takes George to mean George and that is identity thought deluxe. Mother says, "I hate George!" "That means Junior," says the engram, though Mother meant Father.

keyed in: restimulated. The environment around the awake but fatigued or distressed individual is itself similar to the dormant engram. At that moment the engram becomes active.

kinesthesia: the sensation of position, movement, tension, etc., of parts of the body.

Lake Tanganyika: lake in central Africa, between Zaire and Tanzannia. The longest freshwater lake in the world, about 450 miles long, 30–40 miles wide.

laudable: deserving praise; praiseworthy; commendable.

lay: not belonging to, connected with or proceeding from a profession.

leech: one who clings to another for personal gain, especially without giving anything in return, and usually with the implication or effect of exhausting the other's resources; parasite.

Little Beaver: the name of a Navaho orphan adopted by a cowboy named Red Rider, characters in a nationally syndicated comic strip by Fred Harmon. Little Beaver became a radio show in 1942.

little tin soldiers and angels with golden hair: a reference to the poem *Little Boy Blue* by Eugene Field (1850–95), American poet and journalist, known for his children's verse.

lock: a mental image picture of a nonpainful but disturbing experience the person has had, which depends for its force on earlier secondaries and engrams which the experience has restimulated (stirred up).

manic-depressive: is an individual who, because of a phrase or an effort or a restimulation—no more and no less—climbs way up the Tone Scale; and he hits a small peak and then dives off it again and goes on with the engram.

mantle: something that covers, envelops or conceals.

mawkish: characterized by a sickly sentimentality; weakly emotional; maudlin.

Mentholatum: a brand name for a mentholated salve used as a chest rub for colds or flu.

Mest Processing: processing which deals with the root of aberration and physical condition by calling for physical manifestation rather than words. Mest Processing reaches into that strata underlying language and processes the individual in the physical universe. It processes his communication lines directed toward matter, energy, space and time.

mitigated: lessened in force or severity.

mores: folkways that are considered conducive to the welfare of society and so, through general observance, develop the force of law, often becoming part of the formal legal code.

narcoanesthesia: *narco-* meaning sleep and *anesthesia* meaning without feeling. Together this refers to an anesthesia that puts the patient to sleep.

ne plus ultra: Latin, the utmost limit, or the highest point of perfection.

necessity level: a person's ability to rise above his aberrations when his action is required to handle an immediate and serious threat to his survival.

neurotic: characterizing one who is insane or disturbed on some subject (as opposed to a psychotic person, who is just insane in general).

obstetrician: a doctor who specializes in obstetrics, branch of medicine and surgery concerned with treating women before, in and after childbirth.

omniscience: quality or state of having complete or unlimited knowledge, awareness or understanding; perceiving all things.

onerous: burdensome, oppressive or troublesome; causing hardship.

osteopath: a person who specializes in osteopathy, the treatment of disease chiefly by manipulation of the bones and muscles. Osteopathy also includes all types of medical and physical therapy. Osteopathy is based on the concept that the structure and functions of a body and its organs are interdependent and any structural deformity may lead to functional breakdown.

patent: readily open to notice or observation; evident; obvious.

periphery: surrounding space or area; outer parts; environs or outskirts.

pernicious: causing insidious harm or ruin; ruinous; injurious; hurtful.

phenobarbital: a white crystalline powder used as a sedative, a hypnotic and as an antispasmodic in epilepsy.

pickup: a small device attached to the end of a phonograph tone arm that contains a stylus and the mechanism that translates the movement of the stylus in a record groove into a changing electrical voltage.

Plasticine: a brand name for a synthetic material used as a substitute for clay or wax in modeling.

postulates: things put there as a reality.

precipitate: done or made without sufficient deliberation; overhasty; rash.

Preventive Dianetics: that branch of Dianetics based on the principle that engrams can be held to minimal content or prevented entirely, with large gains in favor of mental health and physical well-being as well as social adjustment.

profaned: treated (sacred things) with irreverence or contempt.

propriety: conformity to established standards of good or proper behavior or manners.

psychology: a cult which rose and expired in the first half of the twentieth century.

psychometric: of or having to do with *psychometry*, the measurement of the duration, force, interrelations, or other aspects of mental processes, as by psychological tests.

psychosomatic: *psycho* refers to mind and *somatic* refers to body; the term *psychosomatic* means the mind making the body ill or illnesses which have been created physically within the body by derangement of the mind.

psychotic: an individual who is out of contact to a thorough extent with his present-time environment and who does not compute into the future. He may be an acute psychotic wherein he becomes psychotic for only a few minutes at a time and only occasionally in certain environments (as in rages or apathies) or he may be a chronic psychotic, or in a continual disconnection with the future and present. Psychotics who are dramatically harmful to others are considered dangerous enough to be put away. Psychotics who are harmful on a less dramatic basis are no less harmful to their environment and are no less psychotic.

push-buttons: items, words, phrases, subjects or areas that are easily restimulatable in an individual by the words or actions of other people, and which cause him discomfort, embarrassment or upset, or make him laugh uncontrollably.

rampant: in full sway; prevailing or unchecked.

reactive mind: that portion of a person's mind which works on a totally stimulus-response basis, which is not under his volitional control and which exerts force and the power of command over his awareness, purposes, thoughts, body and actions. The reactive mind is where engrams are stored. Also called **bank.**

recapitulation: the theory that the stages an organism passes through during its embryonic development repeat the evolutionary stages of structural change in its ancestral lineage.

reduction: the act of taking all the charge or pain out of an incident.

remonstrance: the act of speaking, reasoning or pleading in complaint or protest.

Repetitive Straightwire: attention called to an incident over and over amongst other incidents until it is desensitized. Used on conclusions or incidents which do not easily surrender. *See also* **Straightwire** in this Glossary.

restimulate: trigger; stir up.

return: go into a past period. A person can "send" a portion of his mind to a past period on either a mental or combined mental and physical basis and can reexperience incidents which have taken place in his past in the same fashion and with the same sensations as before.

reverie: a light state of "concentration" which the preclear is placed in, not to be confused with hypnosis; in reverie the person is fully aware of what is taking place.

reviling: calling bad names; abusing with words.

rompers: a loose, one-piece garment combining a shirt or blouse and short, bloomerlike pants, worn by young children.

saving grace: a quality that makes up for other generally negative characteristics; redeeming feature.

schizophrenics: *(psychiatry)* originally meaning *split mind*, it has come to denote a psychiatric classification of people whose thoughts and emotions are disassociated from each other.

scintilla: a minute particle; spark; trace.

second dynamic: the urge toward survival through sex or children. This dynamic actually has two divisions. Second dynamic (a) is the sexual act itself, and second dynamic (b) is the family unit, including the rearing of children.

secondary: a period of anguish brought about by a major loss or threat of loss to the individual. The secondary engram depends for its strength and force upon physical-pain engrams which underlie it.

sedulously: in a manner diligent in application or attention.

self-determinism: that state of being wherein the individual can or cannot be controlled by his environment according to his own choice. He is confident about any and all abilities or talents he may possess. He is confident in his interpersonal relationships. He reasons but does not need to react.

semanticists: persons concerned with the meanings or interpretations of the meanings of words, signs, sentences, etc.

seven-league step: a step taken in seven-league boots, fairy-tale boots enabling the wearer to reach seven leagues at a stride. Figuratively, a *seven-league step* is significant forward progress.

shy: throw with a swift, sudden movement.

somatic shut-off: a condition wherein a somatic may be shut off in an incident or elsewhere, either by earlier command or late by painful emotion. There is a whole species of commands which *shut off* pain and emotion simultaneously: this is because the word *feel* is homonymic. "I can't feel anything" is the standard, but the command varies widely and is worded in a great many ways.

somatic strip: a physical indicator mechanism which has to do with time. The auditor orders the somatic strip. The somatic strip can be sent back to the beginning of an engram and will go there. The somatic strip will advance through an engram in terms of minutes counted off by the auditor, so that the auditor can say that the somatic strip will go to the beginning of the engram, then to the point five minutes after the engram began, and so forth.

standard banks: recordings of everything perceived throughout the lifetime up to present time by the individual except physical pain, which is not recorded in the analytical mind but is recorded in the reactive mind.

stimuli: things that incite to action or exertion or quicken action, feeling, thought, etc.

Straightwire: the name of a process. It is the act of stringing a line between present time and some incident in the past, and stringing that line directly and without any detours. The auditor is stringing a straight "wire" of memory between the actual genus (origin) of a condition and present time, thus demonstrating that there is a difference of time and space in the condition then and the condition now, and that the preclear, conceding this difference, then rids himself of the condition or at least is able to handle it.

suppressor: the exterior forces which reduce the chances of the survival of any form.

sympathy computations: computations which make the patient "want to be sick." Sickness has a high survival value says the reactive mind, so it tailors up a body to be sick. For example, if a patient had a tough engramic background, then broke his leg and got sympathy, he thereafter tends to go around with a simulated broken leg—arthritis, etc., etc.

take: to endure or submit to with equanimity or without an appreciable weakening of one's resistance.

tantamount: equivalent, as in value, force, effect or signification.

tempera: a painting medium in which pigment is mixed with water-soluble glutinous materials.

theta–MEST theory: the theory which states that theta, or life, is impinged upon the physical universe and that these two things together, theta and MEST interacting, give us life forms.

thyroid: concerning the thyroid gland, an important ductless gland in the neck of vertebrates, near the larynx and upper windpipe, that affects growth and metabolism.

tomes: books, especially very heavy, large or learned books.

Tone Scale: a scale which shows the emotional tones of a person. These, ranged from the highest to the lowest, are, in part, serenity, enthusiasm (as we proceed downward), conservatism, boredom, antagonism, anger, covert hostility, fear, grief, apathy.

unanimity: complete accord or agreement; being unanimous.

urchins: mischievous boys.

vagaries: unpredictable or erratic actions, occurrences, courses or instances.

valence: personality. The term is used to denote the borrowing of the personality of another. A valence is a substitute for self taken on after the fact of lost confidence in self. A preclear "in his father's valence" is acting as though he were his father.

Validation Processing: processing in which the auditor, at least for one session, concentrates exclusively on the theta side of lock chains, not allowing the preclear to run any but analytical moments on any given subject. When the preclear encounters too much entheta on a given chain, the auditor takes him to analytical moments on another subject (which moments constitute, of course, a parallel chain to the locks on that subject) obtained from the file clerk. During this type of processing, somatics will turn on and off, sometimes severely, but the auditor ignores them, and keeps bringing the preclear back to analytical (not necessarily pleasure) moments.

Vaseline: a brand name for a petroleum jelly product.

veritable: having all the qualities or attributes of the specified person or thing.

vitiated: debased; corrupted; perverted.

wan: showing or suggesting ill health, fatigue, unhappiness, etc.

Index

Aberration, 43, 208
ability, 241, 243
accident prone, 12
adult(s),
> communication between child and, 124
> dramatizations of, 132
> has certain rights around children, 2, 11
> processing adults in child's vicinity, 93

affection, no child ever spoiled by, 52
affinity,
> establishing affinity with child, 80
> importance of, 64
> valences and, 35

afraid, child chronically afraid, 58
age flash, 68
allies,
> ally-forming phrases, 98
> computations, 26
> grandparents as, 59

American Medical Association, 2
analytical experience, 29
analytical mind, described, 15
anxiety, of child, 7–8
ARC triangle, 209
assist, for injury, 99
assists, to remembering, 249–50
attention, child's, 102, 123
auditor, 35, 64, 106
Auditor's Code, 239–40

bad boy, handling for, 50

basic personality, 25
bed-wetting, 79
behavior, 3, 17
birth, silence during, 234
birth engram, examples, 47

case histories, 177–201
Cesarean section, 46
child, children,
> ability to establish affinity with, 80
> adult rights and, 2, 11
> ages when children can be processed, 77
> anxiety of, 7–8
> avoiding restimulation of child, 101
> avoid language in child's reactive bank, 78
> best pattern of processing for, 12
> best therapy for, 2
> chronically afraid, 58
> communication between adults and, 124
> concept of death, 85
> contribution and child revolt, 9
> control and child raising, 4
> defined, 2
> denied responsibility, 53
> don't talk around sick child, 48
> duty of, 11
> education and, 211
> education of children in Dianetics, 33
> efforts to mold, train or control, 7
> factors in child processing, 90

child, children, *(cont.)*
freedom for, 8
future and, 205
getting child's attention, 102
goal of, 11, 53
handling child stuck in
dramatization, 109
handling chronic somatic in child,
115
handling unmanageable child, 108
having child draw pictures, 105
high sense of reality, 54–55
how children return, 33
how to raise, 6
interference with child's decisions,
57
key-ins and health of, 83
laws which apply to behavior of, 3
length of time for processing child,
88
main problem with, 2
natural affection of child for
parents, 52
natural sense of dignity, 80
needs security, 11
no child ever spoiled by affection,
52
parents and child's processing, 82
poems upsetting to, 58
processing adults in child's vicinity,
93
psychotics, schizophrenics and, 36
punishment of, 49
quarrels in vicinity of, 50
reality vs. adult's, 55
regarded as a special branch of
Dianetics, 22
returning in a child, 80
revenge is standard child behavior,
3
rights of, 3, 8
robbed of independence, 57
running pleasure moments on
child, 110
safety for the child's possessions, 8
safety of environment of, 3
self-determinism and possessions
of, 4
sensitive to unreality, 55
sessions with, 137–73
setting up child's own time, 125
society and, 52

child, children, *(cont.)*
span of attention, 123
steps in the processing of children,
78
Straight Memory work with
children, 103
stuck in a valence, 37
tone level of a child, 126
understanding of family operation,
10
valences and affinity of, 35
vocabulary of, 32
with blocked perceptic recalls, 212
child care, Dianetics in, 97, 112
Child Dianetics, 1, 83
childhood illnesses, 26
chronic somatic, 115
Clear, 20, 25
commands in engrams, 26
communication, 64, 124
contagion of aberration, 43, 44
contribution, 8, 9
control, 4, 7
control circuits, 210

death, child's concept of, 85
decisions, preventing child from
making, 57
Dianetics,
aim of, 25
basic principles, 15
children grasp Dianetics easily, 89
children as a special branch of, 22
"do's," 213–14
education of children in, 33
first aid, 235
in child care, 97, 112
language and, 241
processing, 235
standard Dianetics technique, 63
why Dianetics works, 6
Dianetics study group, 207
*Dianetics: The Modern Science of
Mental Health,* 22, 216
dignity of child, 80
discipline, 208, 209
dope-off, 67
dramatizations, 109, 132, 216
duty of child, 11

education,
    benefit of, 56
    children and, 211
    for parents in Child Dianetics, 83
    in Dianetics, 33
    in Preventive Dianetics, 84
    results of education with child, 91
    why education is necessary, 10
Educational Dianetics, 234
energy, of thought, 244
engram(s), 21, 26, 48
environment, 3, 242, 243
ex-barbers, 2

family, 10
family relations, 208
file clerk, 68, 70
first aid, 235
freedom, for child 8
future, children and, 205

game, 109, 130
geometric progression, 43
goal of child, 11, 53, 54
grandparents, 59
guidance centers, 219–29

health, 83, 243

illnesses, 26, 48
imagination, 89
independence, child robbed of, 57
injury, 99

Jesuits, 2
Junior cases, 36

key-in, 46, 48
key-ins, 83

labor, 234
language, 78, 241, 245
laws, which apply to children, 3
life energy, 241
locks, 39, 79, 110

memory, 18, 130

natural affection, 52
natural childbirth, 98
necessity level, 44
nightmares, 107

operations, 26
organisms, 241

parent(s),
    child's dramatizations, 216
    child's processing and, 82
    education for parents in Child
        Dianetics, 83, 84
    example of restimulation from
        parents, 206
    freedom for, 8
    natural affection of child for, 52
    result of undermining parent, 87
perceptic recalls, 212
phrases, 98
physical universe, 241
pictures, 105
play, why play is necessary, 10
playground workshop, 212
pleasure moments, 110
poems, 58
possessions, 4, 8
preclear, 20, 64, 67
prenatal engrams, 130
Preventive Dianetics, 46, 84, 133, 233
processing,
    adults in child's vicinity, 93
    ages children can be processed, 77
    don't make processing a
        punishment, 215
    factors in child processing, 90
    length of time for processing child,
        88
    parents and child's processing, 82
    steps in processing of children, 78
    Tone Scale and, 129
    to use on a child, 12
    use of imagination in, 89
    ways of processing child, 81
psychology, 5, 6
psychosomatic ills, 17
psychotics, 36
punishment, 49, 51, 215

quarrels, 50

reactive mind,
    activity of, 19
    avoid language in child's reactive
        bank, 78
    consists of, 18

Books and Tapes
by L. Ron Hubbard

Dianetics Graduate Books

You've read *Child Dianetics.* Now get the rest of the Dianetics Graduate Books Package. These books by L. Ron Hubbard give you detailed knowledge of how the mind works—data you can use to help yourself and others break out of the traps of life. While you can get these books individually, the Dianetics Graduate Books Package can also be purchased as a set, complete with an attractive slipcase.

Science of Survival • If you ever wondered how people act the way they do, you'll find this book a wealth of information. It's vital to anyone who wants to understand others and improve personal relationships. *Science of Survival* is built around a remarkable chart—The Hubbard Chart of Human Evaluation. With it you can understand and predict other people's behavior and reactions and greatly increase your control over your own life. This is a valuable handbook that can make a difference between success and failure on the job and in life.

Dianetics 55! • Your success in life depends on your ability to communicate. Do you know a formula exists for communication? Learn the rules of better communication that can help you live a more fulfilling life. Here, L. Ron Hubbard deals with the fundamental principles of communication and how you can master these to achieve your goals.

Advanced Procedure and Axioms • For the *first* time the basics of thought and the physical universe have been codified into a set of fundamental laws, signaling an entirely new way to view and approach the subjects of man, the physical universe and even life itself.

Handbook for Preclears • Written as an advanced personal workbook, *Handbook for Preclears* contains easily done processes to help you overcome the effect of times you were not in control of your life, times that your emotions were a barrier to your success and much more. Completing all the fifteen auditing steps contained in this book sets you up for really being in *control* of your environment and life.

Notes on the Lectures of L. Ron Hubbard • Compiled from his fascinating lectures given shortly after the publication of *Dianetics*, this book contains some of the first material Ron ever released on the ARC triangle and the Tone Scale, and how these discoveries relate to auditing.

Basic Dianetics Books

The Basic Dianetics Books Package is your complete guide to the inner workings of the mind. You can get all of these books individually or in a set, complete with an attractive slipcase.

Dianetics: The Modern Science of Mental Health • Acclaimed as the most effective self-help book ever published. Dianetics technology has helped millions reach new heights of freedom and ability. Millions of copies are sold every year! Discover the source of mental barriers that prevent you from achieving your goals—and how to handle them!

The Dynamics of Life • Break through the barriers to your happiness. This is the first book Ron wrote detailing the startling principles behind Dianetics—facts so powerful they can change forever the way you look at yourself and your potentials. Discover how you can use the powerful basic principles in this book to blast through the barriers of your mind and gain full control over your success, future and happiness.

Self Analysis • The complete do-it-yourself handbook for anyone who wants to improve their abilities and success potential. Use the simple, easy-to-learn techniques in *Self Analysis* to build self-confidence and reduce stress.

Dianetics: The Evolution of a Science • It is estimated that we use less than ten percent of our mind's potential. What stops us from developing and using the full potential of our minds? *Dianetics: The Evolution of a Science* is L. Ron Hubbard's incredible story of how he discovered the reactive mind and how he developed the keys to unlock its secrets. Get this firsthand account of what the mind really is, and how you can release its hidden potential.

Basic Scientology Books

The Basic Scientology Books Package contains the knowledge you need to be able to improve conditions in life. These books are available individually or as a set, complete with an attractive slipcase.

Scientology: The Fundamentals of Thought • Improve life *and* make a better world with this easy-to-read book that lays out the fundamental truths about life and thought. No such knowledge has ever before existed, and no such results have ever before been attainable as those which can be reached by the use of this knowledge. Equipped with this book alone, one could perform seeming miracles in changing the states of health, ability and intelligence of people. This *is* how life works. This *is* how you change men, women and children for the better, and attain greater personal freedom.

A New Slant on Life • Have you ever asked yourself who am I? What am I? This book of articles by L. Ron Hubbard answers these all too common questions. This is knowledge one can use every day—for a new, more confident and happier slant on life!

The Problems of Work • Work plays a big part in the game of life. Do you really enjoy your work? Are you certain of your job security? Would you like the increased personal satisfaction of doing your work well? This is the book that shows exactly how to achieve these things and more. The game of life—and within it, the game of work—can be enjoyable and rewarding.

Scientology 0-8: The Book of Basics • What is life? Did you know an individual can create space, energy and time? Here are the basics of life itself, and the secrets of becoming cause over any area of your life. Discover how you can use the data in this book to achieve your goals.

Basic Dictionary of Dianetics and Scientology • Compiled from the works of L. Ron Hubbard, this convenient dictionary contains the terms and expressions needed by anyone learning Dianetics and Scientology technology. And a *special bonus*—an easy-to-read Scientology Organizing Board chart that shows you who to contact for services and information at your nearest Scientology Organization.

OT Library Package

All the following books contain the knowledge of a spiritual being's relationship to this universe and how his abilities to operate successfully in it can be restored. You can get all of these books individually or in a set, complete with an attractive slipcase.

Scientology 8-80 • What are the laws of life? We are all familiar with physical laws such as the law of gravity, but what laws govern life and thought? L. Ron Hubbard answers the riddles of life and its goals in the physical universe.

Scientology 8-8008 • Get the basic truths about your nature as a spiritual being and your relationship to the physical universe around you. Here, L. Ron Hubbard describes procedures designed to increase your abilities to heights previously only dreamed of.

Scientology: A History of Man • A fascinating look at the evolutionary background and history of the human race. This was Ron's first book on the vast time track of man. As Ron said, "This is a cold-blooded and factual account of your last sixty trillion years."

The Creation of Human Ability • This book contains processes designed to restore the power of a thetan over his own postulates, to understand the nature of his beingness, to free his self-determinism and much, much more.

The Phoenix Lectures • Containing L. Ron Hubbard's most complete discussion of the Scientology Axioms, *The Phoenix Lectures* gives you the full knowledge of the basic agreements which make up the very nature of the universe we live in.

The E-Meter Books Package

The following books on the E-Meter give all the data you need to understand and professionally operate your E-Meter.

You can get all of these books individually or in a set, complete with an attractive slipcase.

Introducing the E-Meter • This is a basic book that introduces you to the E-Meter spiritual counseling device and its operation.

Understanding the E-Meter • A large, illustrated book that fully explains the basics of the E-Meter device, how it works and how it can measure the electrical activity of thought. Any question on the principles of the E-Meter can be answered with this book.

E-Meter Essentials • This book gives more advanced aspects of E-Meter use, plus a detailed description of the different types of meter reads on the meter and what they mean.

The Book of E-Meter Drills • With this book you learn all phases of E-Meter operation with detailed, hands-on drills.

Other Scientology Books

Purification: An Illustrated Answer to Drugs • Do toxins and drugs hold down your ability to think clearly? What is the Purification Program and how does it work? How can harmful chemical substances be gotten out of the body? Our society is ridden by abuse of drugs, alcohol and medicine that reduce one's ability to think clearly. Find out what can be done in this introduction to the Purification Program.

All About Radiation • Can the effects of radiation exposure be avoided or reduced? What exactly would happen in the event of an atomic explosion? Get the answers to these and many other questions in this illuminating book. *All About Radiation* describes observations and discoveries concerning the physical and mental effects of radiation and the possibilities for handling them. Get the real facts on the subject of radiation and its effects.

Have You Lived Before This Life? • This is the book that sparked a flood of interest in the ancient puzzle: Does man live only one life? The answer lay in mystery, buried until L. Ron Hubbard's researches unearthed the truth. Actual case histories of people recalling past lives in auditing tell the tale.

Mission Into Time • Here is a fascinating account of a unique research expedition into both space and time, locating physical evidence of past lives in an area rich with history—the Mediterranean. Read Ron's story of the exploration of locations recalled from previous lives!

Dianetics and Scientology Technical Dictionary • This dictionary is your indispensable guide to the words and ideas of Scientology and Dianetics technologies—technologies which can help you increase your know-how and effectiveness in life. Over three thousand words are defined—including a new understanding of vital words like *life, love* and *happiness* as well as Scientology terms.

Modern Management Technology Defined: Hubbard Dictionary of Administration and Management • Here's a real breakthrough in the subject of administration and management! Eighty-six hundred words are defined for greater understanding of any business situation. Clear, precise Scientology definitions describe many previously baffling phenomena and bring truth, sanity and understanding to the often murky field of business management.

How to Live Though an Executive • What are the factors in business and commerce which, if lacking, can keep a person overworked and worried, keep labor and management at each other's throats, and make an unsafe working atmosphere? L. Ron Hubbard reveals principles based on years of research into many different types of organizations.

Introduction to Scientology Ethics • A complete knowledge of ethics is vital to anyone's success in life. Without knowing and applying the information in this book, success is only a matter of luck or chance. That is not much to look forward to. This book contains the answers to questions like, "How do I know when a decision is right or wrong?" "How can I predictably improve things around me?" The powerful ethics technology of L. Ron Hubbard is your way to ever-increasing survival.

Organization Executive Course • The *Organization Executive Course* volumes contain organizational technology never before known to man. This is not just how a Scientology organization works; this is how the operation of *any* organization, *any* activity, can be improved. A person knowing the data in these volumes fully, and applying it, could completely reverse any downtrend in a company—or even a country!

Management Series Volume 1 and 2 • These books contain technology that anyone who works with management in any way must know completely to be a true success. Contained in these books are such subjects as data evaluation, the technology of how to organize any area for maximum production and expansion, how to handle personnel, the actual technology of public relations and much more.

Background and Ceremonies of the Church of Scientology • Discover the beautiful and inspiring ceremonies of the Church of Scientology, and its fascinating religious and historical background. This book contains the illuminating Creed of the Church, church services, sermons and ceremonies, many as originally given in person by L. Ron Hubbard, Founder of Scientology.

What Is Scientology? • Scientology applied religious philosophy has attracted great interest and attention since its beginning. What is Scientology philosophy? What can it accomplish—and why are so many people from all walks of life proclaiming its effectiveness? Find the answers to these questions and many others in *What Is Scientology?*

Introductory and Demonstration Processes and Assists • How can you help someone increase his enthusiasm for living? How can you improve someone's self-confidence on the job? Here are basic Scientology processes you can use to help others deal with life and living.

Volunteer Minister's Handbook • This is a big, practical how-to-do-it book to give a person the basic knowledge on how to help self and others through the rough spots in life. It consists of twenty-one sections—each one covering important situations in life, such as drug and alcohol problems, study difficulties, broken marriages, accidents and illnesses, a failing business, difficult children, and much more. This is the basic tool you need to help someone out of troubles, and bring about a happier life.

Research and Discovery Series • These volumes contain that only existing day-to-day, week-to-week record of the progress of L. Ron Hubbard's research in Dianetics and Scientology. Through the pages of these beautiful volumes you follow L. Ron Hubbard's fantastic research adventure, beginning in the depths of man's degradation and obsession with the material universe and soaring to the realms of the spirit, freed from the bondage of the past.

Technical Bulletins • These volumes contain all of L. Ron Hubbard's technical bulletins and issues from the earliest to the latest. Almost any technical question can be answered from the pages of these volumes, which also include an extremely extensive master subject index.

The Classic Cassettes Series

There are nearly three thousand recorded lectures by L. Ron Hubbard on the subjects of Dianetics and Scientology. What follows is a sampling of these lectures, each known and loved the world over. All of the Classic Cassettes are presented in Clearsound state-of-the-art sound-recording technology, notable for its clarity and brilliance of reproduction.

The Story of Dianetics and Scientology • In this lecture, L. Ron Hubbard shares with you his earliest insights into human nature and gives a compelling and often humorous account of his experiences. Spend an unforgettable time with Ron as he talks about the start of Dianetics and Scientology!

The Road to Truth • The road to truth has eluded man since the beginning of time. In this classic lecture, L. Ron Hubbard explains what this road actually is and why it is the only road one MUST travel all the way once begun. This lecture reveals the only road to higher levels of living.

Scientology and Effective Knowledge • Voyage to new horizons of awareness! *Scientology and Effective Knowledge* by L. Ron Hubbard can help you understand more about yourself and others. A fascinating tale of the beginnings of Dianetics and Scientology.

The Deterioration of Liberty • What do governments fear so much in a population that they amass weapons to defend themselves from people? Find out from Ron in this classic lecture.

Man's Relentless Search • Learn about man's search for himself and his true nature. Find out where this search led and how through Ron's work we have achieved a knowledge of man's true self.

Power of Choice and Self-Determinism • Man's ability to determine the course of his life depends on his ability to exercise his power of choice. Find how you can increase your power of choice and self-determinism in life from Ron in this lecture.

Scientology and Ability • Ron points out that this universe is here because we perceive it and agree to it. Applying Scientology principles to life can bring new adventure to life and put you on the road to discovering better beingness.

The Road to Perfection • Find out what perfection really is and how Scientology gives you the means to attain it.

The Hope of Man • Various men in history brought forth the idea that there was hope of improvement. But L. Ron Hubbard's discoveries in Dianetics and Scientology have made that hope a reality. Find out by listening to this lecture how Scientology has become man's one, true hope for his final freedom.

The Dynamics • In this lecture Ron gives incredible data on the dynamics: how man creates on them, what happens when a person gets stuck in just one; how wars relate to the third dynamic and much more.

Health and Certainty • Ron talks in this classic lecture about the effect false certainty can bring about in an individual and how real certainty is achieved.

Miracles • What are miracles? How do they come about? Find out how things that used to pass as miracles have become just the expected results of Dianetics and Scientology.

My Philosophy • Three dramatic essays by Ron—"My Philosophy," "The Aims of Scientology" and "A Description of Scientology"—come alive for you in this cassette. These powerful writings, beautifully read and set to new and inspiring music, tell you what Scientology is, what it does and what its aims are.

More advanced books and lectures are available. Contact your nearest organization or write directly to the publisher for a full catalog.

Improve Your Life
with Dianetics Graduate
Extension Courses

Dianetics Graduate Books by L. Ron Hubbard give you the knowledge of how the mind works and how you can use that data to help yourself and others to break out of the traps of life. The Dianetics Graduate Extension Courses enable you to increase your application of the information contained in L. Ron Hubbard's books and make this a saner world for all.

Each extension course package includes a lesson book with easy-to-understand instructions and all the lessons you will need to complete it. Each course can be done in the comfort of your own home or right in your local Scientology organization. Your Extension Course Supervisor will review each lesson as you complete it (or mail it in if you do the course at home) and get the results right back to you. When you complete the course you get a beautiful certificate, suitable for framing.

Child Dianetics Extension Course

In 1951 Ron wrote in the introduction to *Child Dianetics*:

"The American Medical Association lately came out with a pamphlet which was called 'How to Control Your Child.' That's just what you don't want to do."

There *is* a correct way to have a successful relationship with children. Enroll on the *Child Dianetics Extension Course* and learn the workable way to get healthy, happier and more successful children. A "must" for any parent or teacher.

Science of Survival Extension Course

Science of Survival was written around a remarkable chart that lays out all the characteristics of human behavior—the Hubbard Chart of Human Evaluation. To learn more about what lies behind the emotional tone levels of others, how you predict how they will react and how to handle them, do the *Science of Survival Extension Course!*

Handbook for Preclears Extension Course

L. Ron Hubbard wrote this book in 1951 in response to the need for an advanced personal workbook. People who follow the exact steps laid out in this book achieve definite, positive changes in the conditions in their lives. Find out what you CAN do about the conditions in your life. Enroll on the *Handbook for Preclears Extension Course* today!

Dianetics 55! Extension Course

Dianetics 55! forms an excellent bridge from the study of the mind to the study of knowledge in its fullest sense—Scientology. Doing the extension course for this book can help you grasp the tremendous amount of important data it contains so you can better apply this information to your benefit.

Advanced Procedure and Axioms Extension Course

For the *first* time the basics of thought and the physical universe have been codified into a set of fundamental laws, signaling an entirely new way to view and approach the subjects of man, the physical universe and even life itself. Gain a full understanding of postulates, self-determinism and *full* responsibility on the *Advanced Procedure and Axioms Extension Course.*

The Notes on the Lectures Extension Course

The physical universe and the universe of thought are two different universes that can have profound effects on an individual's ability to survive or succumb. Learn how Dianetics processing works to bring a person up out of the turbulence of the physical universe to the point of being able to create in life, on all dynamics. Find out more about people—why they are what they are.

Enroll on a Dianetics Graduate Extension Course Today!

For information and enrollment and prices for these Extension Courses and the books they accompany, contact the Public Registrar at your nearest Church of Scientology. (A complete list of Scientology Churches and Organizations is provided at the back of this book.)

Get and start a Dianetics Graduate Extension Course today!

Get Your Free Catalog of Knowledge on How to Improve Life

L. Ron Hubbard's books and tapes increase your ability to understand yourself and others. His works give you the practical know-how you need to improve your life and the lives of your family and friends.

Many more materials by L. Ron Hubbard are available than have been covered in the pages of this book. A free catalog of these materials is available on request.

Write for your free catalog today!

Bridge Publications, Inc.
4751 Fountain Avenue
Los Angeles, California 90029

New Era Publications International, ApS
Store Kongensgade 55
1264 Copenhagen K, Denmark

Apply for Your International Association Membership Today!

The International Association of Scientologists invites you to apply for your annual or lifetime membership today.

The purpose of the International Association of Scientologists is:

"to unite, advance, support and protect Scientology and Scientologists in all parts of the world so as to achieve the aims and purposes of Scientology."

Benefits extended to International Association members include:

* The right to be awarded and hold in force certificates for Scientology and Dianetics training, internship and processing services successfully completed
* Eligibility for professional rates on processing services
* Eligibility for training scholarship awards
* Eligibility for appointment as a Field Staff Member
* Special rates on membership fees for the "I Want to Go OT" Club
* Special rates on Dianetics and Scientology materials and services —including a 20 percent discount on books, tapes and E-Meters.

These benefits are now available only to members of the International Association of Scientologists.

A free six-month membership is extended to beginning Scientologists only—those buying their first book or their first training or processing service.

Apply to the Membership Officer at your nearest Church of Scientology today. Or write directly to the *International Association of Scientologists*, c/o Saint Hill Manor, East Grinstead, Sussex, England RH19 4JY.

"I am always happy to hear from my readers."

L. Ron Hubbard

These were the words of L. Ron Hubbard, who was always very interested in hearing from his friends and readers. He made a point of staying in communication with everyone he came in contact with over his fifty-year career as a professional writer, and he had thousands of fans and friends that he corresponded with all over the world.

The publishers of L. Ron Hubbard's works wish to continue this tradition and welcome letters and comments from you, his readers, both old and new.

Additionally, the publishers will be happy to send you information on anything you would like to know about Ron, his extraordinary life and accomplishments and the vast number of books he has written.

Any message addressed to the Author's Affairs Director at Bridge Publications will be given prompt and full attention.

Bridge Publications, Inc.
4751 Fountain Avenue
Los Angeles, California 90029
U.S.A.

Church and Organization Address List

United States of America

Albuquerque
Church of Scientology
8106 Menaul NE
Albuquerque, New Mexico 87110

Ann Arbor
Church of Scientology
301 North Ingalls Street
Ann Arbor, Michigan 48104

Austin
Church of Scientology
2200 Guadalupe
Austin, Texas 78705

Boston
Church of Scientology
448 Beacon Street
Boston, Massachusetts 02115

Buffalo
Church of Scientology
47 West Huron Street
Buffalo, New York 14202

Chicago
Church of Scientology
3011 North Lincoln Avenue
Chicago, Illinois 60657

Cincinnati
Church of Scientology
215 West 4th Street, 5th Floor
Cincinnati, Ohio 45202

Columbus
Church of Scientology
167 East State Street
Columbus, Ohio 43215

Dallas
Church of Scientology
Celebrity Centre Dallas
8501 Manderville Lane
Dallas, Texas 75231

Denver
Church of Scientology
375 South Navajo Street
Denver, Colorado 80223

Detroit
Church of Scientology
321 Williams Street
Royal Oak, Michigan 48067

Honolulu
Church of Scientology
1100 Alakea Street #301
Honolulu, Hawaii 96813

Kansas City
Church of Scientology
3619 Broadway
Kansas City, Missouri 64111

Las Vegas
Church of Scientology
846 East Sahara Avenue
Las Vegas, Nevada 89104

Las Vegas *(cont.)*
Church of Scientology
Celebrity Centre Las Vegas
1100 South 10th Street
Las Vegas, Nevada 89104

Long Island
Church of Scientology
330 Fulton Avenue
Hempstead, New York 11550

Los Angeles and vicinity
Church of Scientology
4810 Sunset Boulevard
Los Angeles, California 90027

Church of Scientology
1451 Irvine Boulevard
Tustin, California 92680

Church of Scientology
263 East Colorado Boulevard
Pasadena, California 91101

Church of Scientology
10335 Magnolia Boulevard
North Hollywood, California 91601

Church of Scientology
American Saint Hill Organization
1413 North Berendo Street
Los Angeles, California 90027

Church of Scientology
American Saint Hill Foundation
1413 North Berendo Street
Los Angeles, California 90027

Church of Scientology
Advanced Organization of
Los Angeles
1306 North Berendo Street
Los Angeles, California 90027

Church of Scientology
Celebrity Centre International
5930 Franklin Avenue
Hollywood, California 90028

Miami
Church of Scientology
120 Giralda Avenue
Coral Gables, Florida 33134

Minneapolis
Church of Scientology
3019 Minnehaha Avenue
Minneapolis, Minnesota 55406

New Haven
Church of Scientology
909 Whalley Avenue
New Haven, Connecticut 06515

New York City
Church of Scientology
227 West 46th Street
New York City, New York 10036

Church of Scientology
Celebrity Centre New York
65 East 82nd Street
New York City, New York 10028

Orlando
Church of Scientology
710-A East Colonial Drive
Orlando, Florida 32803

Philadelphia
Church of Scientology
1315 Race Street
Philadelphia, Pennsylvania 19107

Phoenix
Church of Scientology
4450 North Central Avenue, Suite 102
Phoenix, Arizona 85012

Portland
Church of Scientology
1536 Southeast 11th Avenue
Portland, Oregon 97214

Church of Scientology
Celebrity Centre Portland
709 Southwest Salmon Street
Portland, Oregon 97205

Sacramento
Church of Scientology
825 15th Street
Sacramento, California 95814

San Diego
Church of Scientology
701 "C" Street
San Diego, California 92101

San Francisco
Church of Scientology
83 McAllister Street
San Francisco, California 94102

San Jose
Church of Scientology
3604 Stevens Creek Boulevard
San Jose, California 95117

Santa Barbara
Church of Scientology
524 State Street
Santa Barbara, California 93101

Seattle
Church of Scientology
2004 Westlake Avenue
Seattle, Washington 98121

St. Louis
Church of Scientology
9510 Page Boulevard
St. Louis, Missouri 63132

Tampa
Church of Scientology
4809 North Armenia Avenue, Suite 215
Tampa, Florida 33603

Clearwater
Church of Scientology
Flag® Service Organization
210 South Fort Harrison Avenue
Clearwater, Florida 33516

Washington, DC
Founding Church of Scientology
2125 "S" Street NW
Washington, DC 20008

Canada

Edmonton
Church of Scientology
10349 82nd Avenue
Edmonton, Alberta
Canada T6E 1Z9

Kitchener
Church of Scientology
8 Water Street North
Kitchener, Ontario
Canada N2H 5A5

Montreal
Church of Scientology
4489 Papineau Street
Montréal, Québec
Canada H2H 1T7

Ottawa
Church of Scientology
150 Rideau Street, 2nd Floor
Ottawa, Ontario
Canada K1N 5X6

Quebec
Church of Scientology
226 St-Joseph est
Québec, Québec
Canada G1K 3A9

Toronto
Church of Scientology
696 Yonge Street
Toronto, Ontario
Canada M4Y 2A7

Vancouver
Church of Scientology
401 West Hastings Street
Vancouver, British Columbia
Canada V6B 1L5

Winnipeg
Church of Scientology
Suite 125—388 Donald Street
Winnipeg, Manitoba
Canada R3B 2J4

United Kingdom

Birmingham
Church of Scientology
80 Hurst Street
Birmingham
England B5 4TD

Brighton
Church of Scientology
Dukes Arcade, Top Floor
Dukes Street
Brighton, Sussex
England

East Grinstead
Saint Hill Foundation
Saint Hill Manor
East Grinstead, West Sussex
England RH19 4JY

Advanced Organization Saint Hill
Saint Hill Manor
East Grinstead, West Sussex
England RH19 4JY

Edinburgh
Hubbard Academy of Personal
Independence
20 Southbridge
Edinburgh, Scotland EH1 1LL

London
Church of Scientology
68 Tottenham Court Road
London, W1P 0BB England

Manchester
Church of Scientology
258 Deansgate
Manchester, England M3 4BG

Plymouth
Church of Scientology
41 Ebrington Street
Plymouth, Devon
England PL4 9AA

Sunderland
Church of Scientology
51 Fawcett Street
Sunderland, Tyne and Wear
England SR1 1RS

Austria

Vienna
Church of Scientology
Mariahilfer Strasse 88A/II/2
A-1070 Vienna, Austria

Belgium

Brussels
Church of Scientology
45A, rue de l'Ecuyer
1000 Bruxelles, Belgium

Denmark

Aarhus
Church of Scientology
Guldsmedegade 17, 2
8000 Aarhus C, Denmark

Copenhagen
Church of Scientology
Store Kongensgade 55
1264 Copenhagen K, Denmark

Church of Scientology
Vesterbrogade 23 A – 25
1620 Copenhagen V, Denmark

Church of Scientology
Advanced Organization Saint Hill for
Europe and Africa
Jernbanegade 6
1608 Copenhagen V, Denmark

France

Angers
Church of Scientology
10–12, rue Max Richard
49000 Angers, France

Clermont-Ferrand
Church of Scientology
2 Pte, rue Giscard de la Tour Fondue
63000 Clermont-Ferrand, France

Lyon
Church of Scientology
3, place des Capucins
69001 Lyon, France

Paris
Church of Scientology
65, rue de Dunkerque
75009 Paris, France

Church of Scientology
Celebrity Centre Paris
69, rue Legendre
75017 Paris, France

St. Etienne
Church of Scientology
24, rue Marengo
42000 St. Etienne, France

Germany

Berlin
Church of Scientology e.V.
Sponholzstrasse 51/52
1000 Berlin 41, Germany

Düsseldorf
Church of Scientology
Friedrichstrasse 28
4000 Düsseldorf, West Germany

Frankfurt
Church of Scientology
Darmstadter Landstr. 119–125
6000 Frankfurt/Main, West Germany

Hamburg
Church of Scientology e.V.
Steindamm 63
2000 Hamburg 1, West Germany

Church of Scientology
Celebrity Centre Hamburg
Mönckebergstrasse 5
2000 Hamburg 1
West Germany

Munich
Church of Scientology e.V.
Beichstrasse 12
D-8000 München 40, West Germany

Greece

Athens
Applied Philosophy Center of Greece
  (K.E.F.E.)
Ippokratous 175B
114 72 Athens, Greece

Israel

Tel Aviv
Scientology and Dianetics College
7 Salomon Street
Tel Aviv 66023, Israel

Italy

Brescia
Church of Scientology
Dei Tre Laghi
Via Fratelli Bronzetti N. 20
25125 Brescia, Italy

Milano
Church of Scientology
Via Abetone, 10
20137 Milano, Italy

Monza
Church of Scientology
Via Cavour, 5
20052 Monza, Italy

Novara
Church of Scientology
Corso Cavallotti No. 7
28100 Novara, Italy

Nuoro
Church of Scientology
Corso Garibaldi, 108
08100 Nuoro, Italy

Padua
Church of Scientology
Via Mameli 1/5
35131 Padova, Italy

Pordenone
Church of Scientology
Via Montereale, 10/C
33170 Pordenone, Italy

Rome
Church of Scientology
Via di San Vito, 11
00185 Roma, Italy

Turin
Church of Scientology
Via Guarini, 4
10121 Torino, Italy

Verona
Church of Scientology
Vicolo Chiodo No. 4/A
37121 Verona, Italy

Netherlands

Amsterdam
Church of Scientology
Nieuwe Zijds Voorburgwal 271
1012 RL Amsterdam, Netherlands

Norway

Oslo
Church of Scientology
Storgata 9
0155 Oslo 1, Norway

Portugal

Lisbon
Instituto de Dianética
Rua Actor Taborde 39–4°
1000 Lisboa, Portugal

Spain

Barcelona
Dianética
Calle Pau Claris 85, Principal 1ª
08010 Barcelona, Spain

Madrid
Asociación Civil de Dianética
Montera 20, Piso 2
28013 Madrid, Spain

Sweden

Göteborg
Church of Scientology
Norra Hamngatan 4
S-411 14 Göteborg, Sweden

Malmö
Church of Scientology
Stortorget 27
S-211 34 Malmö, Sweden

Stockholm
Church of Scientology
Kammakargatan 46
S-111 60 Stockholm, Sweden

Switzerland

Basel
Church of Scientology
Herrengrabenweg 56
4054 Basel, Switzerland

Bern
Church of Scientology
Effingerstrasse 25
CH-3008 Bern, Switzerland

Geneva
Church of Scientology
4, rue du Léman
1201 Genève, Switzerland

Lausanne
Church of Scientology
10, rue de la Madeleine
1003 Lausanne, Switzerland

Zürich
Church of Scientology
Badenerstrasse 294
CH-8004 Zürich, Switzerland

Australia

Adelaide
Church of Scientology
24 Waymouth Street
Adelaide, South Australia 5000
Australia

Brisbane
Church of Scientology
2nd Floor, 106 Edward Street
Brisbane, Queensland 4000
Australia

Canberra
Church of Scientology
Suite 16, 108 Bunda Street
Canberra Civic
A.C.T 2601, Australia

Melbourne
Church of Scientology
44 Russell Street
Melbourne, Victoria 3000
Australia

Perth
Church of Scientology
39–41 King Street
Perth, Western Australia 6000
Australia

Sydney
Church of Scientology
201 Castlereagh Street
Sydney, New South Wales 2000
Australia

Church of Scientology
Advanced Organization Saint Hill
 Australia, New Zealand and
 Oceania
19–37 Greek Street
Glebe, New South Wales 2037
Australia

Japan

Tokyo
Scientology Tokyo Org
101 Toyomi Nishi Gotanda Heights
2-13-5 Nishi Gotanda
Shinagawa-Ku
Tokyo, Japan 141

New Zealand

Auckland
Church of Scientology
2nd Floor, 44 Queen Street
Auckland 1, New Zealand

Africa

Bulawayo
Church of Scientology
74 Abercorn Street
Bulawayo, Zimbabwe

Cape Town
Church of Scientology
5 Beckham Street
Gardens
Cape Town 8001, South Africa

Durban
Church of Scientology
57 College Lane
Durban 4001, South Africa

Harare
Church of Scientology
First Floor State Lottery Building
P.O. Box 3524
Corner Speke Avenue and
    Julius Nyerere Way
Harare, Zimbabwe

Johannesburg
Church of Scientology
Security Building, 2nd Floor
95 Commissioner Street
Johannesburg 2001, South Africa

Church of Scientology
101 Huntford Building
40 Hunter Street
Cnr. Hunter & Fortesque Roads
Yeoville 2198
Johannesburg, South Africa

Port Elizabeth
Church of Scientology
2 St. Christopher
27 Westbourne Road
Port Elizabeth 6001, South Africa

Pretoria
Church of Scientology
"Die Meent Arcade," 2nd Level,
    Shop 43b
266 Pretorius Street
Pretoria 0002, South Africa

Latin America

Colombia

Bogotá
Centro Cultural de Dianética
Carrera 19 No. 39–55
Apartado Aereo 92419
Bogotá, D.E. Colombia

Mexico

Estado de México
Instituto Tecnologico de Dianética,
    A.C.
Reforma 530, Lomas
México D.F., C.P. 11000

Guadalajara
Organización Cultural Dianética de
    Guadalajara, A.C.
Av. Lopez Mateos Nte. 329
Sector Hidalgo
Guadalajara, Jalisco, México

Mexico City
Asociación Cultural Dianética, A.C.
Hermes No. 46
Colonia Crédito Constructor
03940 México 19, D.F.

Instituto de Filosofia Aplicada, A.C.
Durango #105
Colonia Roma
06700 México D.F.

Instituto de Filosofia Aplicada, A.C.
Plaza Rio de Janeiro No. 52
Colonia Roma
06700 México D.F.

Organización, Desarrollo y
    Dianética, A.C.
Providencia 1000
Colonia Del Valle
C.P. 03100 México D.F.

Centro de Dianética Polanco
Insurgentes Sur 536, 1er piso
    Esq. Nogales
Colonia Roma Sur C.P.
06700 México D.F.

Venezuela

Valencia
Asociación Cultural Dianética de
    Venezuela, A.C.
Ave. 101 No. 150–23
Urbanizacion La Alegria
Apartado Postal 833
Valencia, Venezuela

To obtain any books or cassettes by L. Ron Hubbard which are not available at your local organization, contact any of the following publishers:

Bridge Publications, Inc.
4751 Fountain Avenue
Los Angeles, California 90029

Continental Publications Liaison Office
696 Yonge Street
Toronto, Ontario
Canada M4Y 2A7

New Era Publications International
  ApS
Store Kongensgade 55
1264 Copenhagen K, Denmark

Era Dinámica Editores, S.A. de C.V.
Alabama 105
Colonia Nápoles
C.P. 03810 México, D.F.

NEW ERA Publications, Ltd.
78 Holmethorpe Avenue
Redhill, Surrey RH1 2NL
United Kingdom

N.E. Publications Australia Pty. Ltd.
2 Verona Street
Paddington, New South Wales 2021
Australia

Continental Publications Pty. Ltd.
P.O. Box 27080
Benrose 2011
South Africa

NEW ERA Publications Italia Srl
Via L.G. Columella, 12
20128 Milano, Italy

NEW ERA Publications GmbH
Otto—Hahn—Strasse 25
6072 Dreieich 1, Germany

NEW ERA Publications France
111, Boulevard de Magenta
75010 Paris, France

New Era Publications España, S.A.
C/De la Paz, 4/1° dcha
28012 Madrid, Spain

New Era Japan
5-4-5-803 Nishigotanda
Shinagawa-Ku
Tokyo, Japan 141